State and Local Government and Politics

The Dickenson Series in Political Science
Edited by John C. Bollens, University of California, Los Angeles

Public Administration
John C. Buechner, University of Colorado

Legislatures in the American Political System
Dean E. Mann, University of California, Santa Barbara

American Foreign Policy in a Polycentric World
Douglas Mendel, University of Wisconsin—Milwaukee

Executives in the American Political System
John C. Ries, University of California, Los Angeles

State and Local Government and Politics
Gerald Rigby, California State Polytechnic College, Kellogg-Voorhis

Courts in the American Political System
Henry J. Schmandt, University of Wisconsin—Milwaukee

Politics: Interest Group Theory
Harry M. Scoble, University of California, Los Angeles

American Political Thought
Duane E. Smith, University of California, Los Angeles

The Current International System
David O. Wilkinson, University of California, Los Angeles

Personality and Politics
E. Victor Wolfenstein, University of California, Los Angeles

State and Local Government and Politics

Gerald Rigby

California State Polytechnic College, Kellogg-Voorhis

Dickenson Publishing Company, Inc., Belmont, California

Contents

Foreword

The books in THE DICKENSON SERIES IN POLITICAL SCIENCE are designed for use together or individually as texts or collateral readings. Each volume, prepared by a knowledgeable scholar, deals with a significant area of political science in a comprehensive, up-to-date, but concise manner. Each is issue oriented and seeks to present a meaningful, stimulating analysis, not mere description. Written in a direct, interesting style intended to inform rather than mystify, each book distills and interprets the best in the literature. A bibliographical essay, which furnishes perspective and guidance for further reading in the field, constitutes an appropriate concluding section.

In writing *State and Local Government and Politics*, Gerald Rigby has selected his materials for their contribution to an understanding of the American state and local political subsystems. By following this procedure, he has avoided engulfing his readers in an endless sea of factual details—a trap into which a state and local book may easily fall because of the almost countless particulars that may be discussed about a subject involving tens of thousands of governments.

Professor Rigby has concentrated on analysis and theoretical concerns rather than organizational minutiae. In a mature but not overly sophisticated way, he has critically examined various major policy questions and provided a framework for the study of politics in the state and local arena.

Gerald Rigby's dual life roles of activist and theorist are evident throughout this volume.

Los Angeles, California   John C. Bollens

Preface

Recent years have brought renewed interest in state and local government and politics, resulting in the publication of many new texts. The present volume is not designed to be simply another rehash of the basic "nuts and bolts" of state and local governments. It is intended to set state and local government and politics in the larger theoretical framework of a systematic analysis of American government and politics. This approach sets the present volume apart from most texts in the field, as the various small volumes designed as supplementary texts often fail to consider the broader political system of which state and local subsystems are parts.

In following this basic purpose, I have attempted to explain clearly, without either oversimplifying or unduly complicating, the basic idea behind considering state and local governments as subsystems of the larger political system, emphasizing how each aspect of state and local government and politics fits into the American political system. Thus, constitutions are discussed within the framework of the nature of constitutionalism, so that their role and characteristics can be understood in relation to constitutions anywhere in the system. Likewise, Chapter 3 is devoted to explaining the nature of democratic politics, so that the discussion of state and local politics in Chapter 4 can be more than a repetition of factual details or a fruitless effort to see similarities without an understanding of the interrelationships of the system. Similarly, the major branches of governments—legislative, executive-administrative, and judicial—are examined as interrelated policymaking agencies. Details on structure and organization are not neglected but simply subordinated to the more important concern for theoretical relevance and the importance of understanding the systematic relationships.

This volume, then, should serve as a basic text for those who wish to approach the study of state and local government as a laboratory for examining the nature and functioning of democratic politics. It should fit well also with larger courses in American government and politics where the emphasis is on development of a theory of democracy rather than mastery of minutiae on structure and function.

The book draws heavily on the work of the many political scientists who have pioneered in development of our understanding of democratic politics generally and state and local politics specifically. To them collectively I am indebted. I am especially indebted to four others whose help has been much more personal: my wife, Barbara, for her encouragement, understanding, and professional assistance; my friend Phillip Cobb, student assistant, for proofreading the manuscript and preparing the index; and Joe Dana, Dickenson political science editor, and Jack Bollens, editor of this series, for seeing the book through from idea to publication.

Diamond Bar, California   Gerald Rigby

1

State and Local Government in the Political System

Both history and tradition assign important roles to state and local government. Historically, the states preexisted the national government and were the repositories of all governing power. Traditionally, we have accepted uncritically the notion that democratic government works best at the "grass roots" level, that smallness and closeness are necessary for legitimacy in the exercise of governmental power.

Some years ago it became popular to predict the demise of state and local government. Even now some still forecast the imminent withering away of these levels of government in the shadow of the colossus of national power. But the facts belie such predictions. Government below the national level has never done so many important things, spent so much money, employed so many people—in short, has never been as vital as it is today.

Importance of State and Local Government

State and local governments are today viable and dynamic partners of the national government in our political system. The evidence leading to this conclusion starts with the obvious—there is no United States independent of the people, areas, and institutions encompassed by the term "state and local." The United States and the states and localities are made up of the same people, living in the same geographic territory, using similar and in many cases identical institutional arrangements. In the language of modern political scientists, state and local governments are subsystems of a larger political system.

There is other evidence to underscore the importance of state and local government. Many of our states and some of our cities are responsible for governing more people than many independent nations. State and local governments are responsible for well over 40 percent of all expenditures for general governmental purposes and about 70 percent of expenditures for domestic purposes. They account for 10 percent of the gross national product, with total purchases of goods and services approximately equal to those of the national government. State and local expenditures have increased well over 100 percent during the last ten years, both absolutely and per capita, a rate closely approximating the increase in federal expenditures for domestic purposes.

If one uses number of employees as a guide, the evidence is equally striking. For instance, state and local governments employ about 75 percent of all those on governmental payrolls. There are over 8 million employees of state and local governments compared with only 2.6 million employees of the national government. Almost half of the federal employees are engaged in defense or international relations activities, while all the state and local government employees are occupied with domestic governmental affairs. Federal government employment has increased slightly less than 10 percent during the last ten years, but state and local employment has grown by almost 60 percent.

Such statistical measures are not the most impressive indices of the importance of state and local governments. The citizen's daily life is affected at least as much by the activities of his state and local governments as by those of the national government. The latter's overriding concern with, among others, national defense, strategic position, and foreign and economic affairs certainly directly affects the citizen. But the activities of state and local governments just as certainly are consequential to him. These levels of government, for example, are responsible for determining most of the criminal law of the land, and for establishing and maintaining a vast network of courts for the settlement of most of the criminal and also civil conflicts in which the citizen might be involved. They are responsible for educating his children, paving the streets, providing for drainage, water supply, electrical power, and public transportation, for regulating, in the interest of his safety, the operation of most businesses, for providing police protection, public health facilities, recreation facilities, and parks, for preservation of order, protection of the citizen's property and life from hoodlums and vandals, and they are also responsible for determining the conditions under which he may drive an automobile, engage in business, or build a house—to list only a few of their functions.

State and local governments are also important to the citizen because of their closeness to him. The connection between democracy and the involvement of people at the local level is very much a part of that catalog of beliefs upon which our democratic processes are built. The closeness of these institutions to the individual makes it imperative that he understand the processes through which he may participate, and that what he sees meets his expectations as to how democratic institutions should operate. At least these governments must avoid contributing to the disillusionment that may result if the citizen sees that they cannot solve the problems facing them. Since over half our population lives in the 15 largest metropolitan areas, the major domestic problems arise there. Our efforts to solve them require dynamic approaches by local government. Indeed, the increased urbanization of American society is perhaps the most significant single factor contributing to the importance of government at the state and local levels.

Finally, but certainly not of least importance, state and local governments play critical roles in the operation of government at the national level. They are the institutional framework upon which Congress and the President rest; national politics is in a real sense a misnomer, for all national politics is built upon the politics of our states and local areas. Furthermore, it is the state and local agencies which administer most federal programs.

In short, then, state and local governments have never been more important in the American political system. They form the framework upon which the federal union is built. They are the citizen's most intimate link to the political system that so affects his life. They are also a laboratory in which, close at hand, we may observe that system in operation.

American Government as a Political System

Traditionally, the study of government and politics has been segmental. Political scientists have concentrated on understanding the legislature, the Presidency, the bureaucracy, the courts, state government, city government, the taxing process, and other individual parts with little or no explicit concern for their interrelationships or the whole to which they belong. In recent years we have begun to recognize that we are examining a political *system*, and that while the individual parts of that system need to and can be understood through a kind of societal vivisection, no one part of an operating system can be separated from the whole without distortion of both, in much the same way that severing the leg of a frog for laboratory examination does something to both the leg and the frog.

System theory is a highly sophisticated and complex approach to the understanding of a political society, one which has engaged the attention of a number of leading political scientists and sociologists and promises to contribute materially to the development of our political knowledge.[1] It is, however, only a tool of analysis and not a substitute for or in itself a theory of politics. What it has contributed mainly is a reorientation of our understanding. The basic presumption is that there is a whole, a system, in which various subsystems can be defined and examined, and that the relationships among these subsystems are orderly, patterned, and predictable. Things do not just happen; their "happening" can be explained, potentially at least, in terms of the interactions within the system, or, as some would have it, as functions of the system. Consequently, the more we know about relationships in the system the better we will understand the things that happen.

In such an approach the emphasis is shifted from the usual study of formal and legal relationships, structural and organizational patterns, and descriptive and prescriptive formulas as explanations of the way the system does or ought to operate. Instead, the effort is to identify and examine observable interactions to divine predictable patterns upon which accurate analysis can rest. *Behavior*, as the basis of these relationships, becomes the focus of the study of a political system, and the way the behavior of one or several parts of the system affects that of others, together with the means through which such interaction takes place, that is, through organizations, structures, rules, laws, and so forth, becomes the concern. Here "roles" are more important to understanding than formal powers, observable relationships more productive than formally declared statutory jurisdictions and responsibilities, explication of the way things really operate more productive for the development of theoretical propositions than normative prescriptions of the way things ought to operate. Knowledge of the factors that determine roles, whether they be attributes of the individual part of the system or external societal determinants, is essential for understanding the parts and the re-

---

[1] See, for example, David Easton, *A Systems Analysis of Political Life* (New York: John Wiley & Sons, Inc., 1965), and Robert A. Dahl, *Modern Political Analysis* (Englewood Cliffs, N.J.: Prentice-Hall, Inc., 1963), especially Chaps. 3, "Political Systems: Similarities," and 4, "Political Systems: Differences." Useful applications are provided in Charles G. Mayo and Beryl L. Crowe, *American Political Parties: A Systematic Perspective* (New York: Harper & Row, Publishers, 1967), Chap. 1, "The Structural-Functional Concept of a Political Party," and in Glendon Schubert, *Judicial Policy-Making* (Glenview, Ill.: Scott, Foresman & Company, 1965), particularly pp. 1–8, "The Political System," and pp. 105–30, "A Systematic Model of Judicial Policy-Making."

lationships among them. However, the formal structural and organizational factors must still be examined, for they are in large part both defined by and definitive of the attributes, attitudes, and roles of the various units of the system.

To understand the American political system we must study the subsystems composing it, but these subsystems can only be understood through understanding the whole system. Obviously, this presents a problem, which can largely be overcome, however, by recognizing its existence. That is, once we realize that a study of state and local governments, or any other part of our political system, cannot be complete without an understanding of how it relates to other subsystems and to the whole, we are well on our way to avoiding simplistic explanations.

State and Local Governments as Political Subsystems

In view of the fact that there are 50 state governments and approximately 80,000 local governmental units, generalizations are dangerous and reliable comparisons difficult. Consider the diversity in over 3,000 counties, 17,000 municipalities, 17,000 townships and towns, and over 40,000 special districts. Each of these governments and the political environment in which it operates constitutes a political subsystem, more notable for its differences from counterpart subsystems than for its similarities. Look at the states, for instance. In area Alaska is some 500 times the size of Rhode Island. In population the states range from approximately 300,000 (Nevada) to about 20 million (California). Some states are almost entirely urban, with practically all their population living in metropolitan centers, while some are mainly rural, with few if any towns of 50,000. There are vast differences in the wealth of states, whether measured by per capita income or mineral deposits and other resources. Topography, weather, employment patterns, and cultural inheritance all vary throughout the states. And vast differences exist in the way in which politics is approached, in attitudes towards government, and in programs and policies adopted.

Although such differences make it difficult to find meaningful comparisons, a study of these subsystems from the standpoint of general theoretical problems can lead to productive exploration of the question of how the American democratic system operates, or more correctly, to the development of an understanding of what the American democratic system is. To conceive of them as subsystems—any other way would make nonsense of the phrase "American political system" —is to suggest that they operate essentially the same, according to

identifiable patterns. To understand the approach of these subsystems to the problems of representation, policymaking, or political
participation, for instance, can take us a great way towards understanding what it means in a democratic system to speak of representation, public policymaking, or democratic participation.

Structural and Organizational Similarities

While recognizing the dissimilarities in the thousands of governmental units in the states, we can also note similarities in these subsystems, particularly in structure and organization. While the names
vary, the kinds of governing units involved differ only slightly. Each
of the state governments has a legislature, a governor, and a system of courts. Even though there is a difference in specific composition
of these institutions, each state separates the powers among these
three major branches of government, and is dedicated in varying degree to maintaining their independence. It is thus possible to speak
of state legislatures, state executives, and state judicial systems without having to consider each one individually. In virtually every state
there is essentially the same kind of organization of local government. The major administrative subdivisions of the state are almost
always counties, and the chief governing units at the local level are
universally municipalities. And in all states there is a network of
special districts, separate governing units with a single function or
a group of closely related ones.

Furthermore, the general pattern for county government is par-
liamentary, that is, a board has both executive and legislative functions (although a limited number of counties have shifted to an
elected or appointed chief executive). And while there are over 18,000
units of government called cities, towns, or (the more general term)
municipalities, they share the three basic structural arrangements in
vogue—the mayor-council system, in which the mayor is elected independently of the council; the commission form, in which both executive and legislative functions are performed by a commission whose
members also serve as the major administrative heads of the functioning departments; and the council-manager form, in which the elected
council hires a city manager, a professional administrator, to carry on
the executive function. Special districts also follow a uniform format,
almost invariably being governed by a plural body independent of
other local or state units.

The mode of selection, the names, and the jurisdictions of the
courts in the various state and local judicial subsystems differ
greatly, but in all of them there is a general approach to the nature of

law and the judicial function that is identifiable throughout the American political system. Likewise, the politics of every state involves an extensive network of quite similar political party structures.

In the following chapters it will become increasingly apparent that the structure, organization, and operating procedures of these subsystems are strikingly similar and suggestive of an overall pattern. It is toward developing an understanding of that pattern, of how the state and local political units interact to make up the nation's political system, that we consider first the basic instruments of government in these subsystems.

Basic Instruments of Government: Constitutions and Constitutionalism

Americans are dedicated to written constitutions. Every level of government and almost every private organization has its own constitution. But a genuine constitution is neither dependent upon nor synonymous with a written document. Constitutionalism can exist without a written document, and can be absent when there is a written constitution. The most that can be said about a written constitution is that it may be useful in establishing a constitutional system and may be evidence of the existence of genuine constitutionalism.

Nature of Constitutions and Constitutionalism

Carl J. Friedrich suggests that a constitution exists when there is constitutionalism, and constitutionalism exists when there is a system of effective restraints on governmental action:

As a political process, the constitution can be described as analagous to the rules of the game insuring fair play. This is the meaning of the word "constitution" in its functional sense, as distinguished from its meaning in law, history, and in medicine. The political scientist inquiring into the process of constitutionalizing a government must study the technique of establishing and maintaining effective restraints on political and governmental action.[2]

Constitutionalism exists when there are regularized restraints on government, whether they are formalized in a written document or not. In this country, by and large, a system of regularized restraints

[2] C. J. Friedrich, *Constitutional Government and Democracy* (New York: Ginn & Company, 1959), p. 26.

on government is reflected both in the requirements of written constitutions and, more importantly, in a societal attitude toward the use of governmental power, in the expectation that government will function in an orderly, predictable, and restrained fashion. This is the real constitution of the United States, and when this societal expectation exists in the states and local communities constitutionalism also exists. Constitutionalism has to do with the spirit, the myths, the actual operative procedures, and the expectations of the people, not simply with the document *per se.*

A look at other countries with constitutions, written and unwritten, supports this approach. Both the United States and France have written constitutions, and although the government of each operates in significantly different fashion, both are constitutional and democratic societies. The Union of Soviet Socialist Republics also has a written constitution, one which many observers agree compares favorably in form with our own. However, the difference in the Soviet Union's experience is significant. In the former two countries constitutionalism exists, whereas in the USSR, it does not. The British have no written constitution, although there are various landmark documents that make up a part of the British constitution. However, there is no doubt that the British operate with regularized restraints on government. In the German Weimar Republic after World War I, a democratically conceived and constructed written document was not enough to guarantee a constitutional government. The experience of our Latin American neighbors with written constitutions, some almost verbatim reproductions of our own, has produced strong evidence that a written constitution alone will not guarantee a constitutional government.

Although every state government operates within the framework of a written constitution, and local governments universally operate within the framework of a constitutional instrument (either a charter, another basic enabling act or a collection of state laws), an examination of these documents will not disclose whether constitutionalism exists. One must ask: Do the provisions of the constitutional documents, when considered together with the way things are actually done, give evidence of the pattern we have defined as constitutionalism—regularized restraints on government such that the people may and do expect it to operate in an orderly, predictable, and restrained fashion?

The Federal Constitution and the States

The Constitution of the United States establishes the basic structural arrangements by which this country is governed. These arrange-

ments include a representative system of government, a skeletal
framework of government, and a federal system. We have emphasized
that the concept of constitutionalism places major emphasis on governmental restraints. It is in this respect that the Constitution, together with the amendments, is most specific, including as it does a
number of restraints on procedure, structure, and activities. There
is a general expectation that the Constitution assures a regularized
governmental process and that its guarantees will be meaningful in
application, not just symbolic. Furthermore, restraints, both formal
and traditional, are sanctioned in the political system through competition for political power. Regardless of the document's language,
public officials must tread lightly in any attempt to exercise exceptional authority, not so much because of the danger of going beyond
their legal authority but because of the repercussions on their political futures. The democratic political process serves both to enforce
and to supplement formal restraints.

The Constitution establishes only a skeletal framework upon which
the enormous governmental machinery of today has gradually been
built. It provides for only three institutions of government—the Congress, the Presidency, and the Supreme Court. It vests legislative
power in the Congress, executive power in the Presidency, and judicial
power in the Supreme Court and such inferior courts as Congress
might establish. The details of that organizational structure, other
than those pertaining to selection, the bicameral structure of Congress, and some congressional procedures, are not included. Nevertheless, this separation of power, through which the three major
branches interact in a kind of "antagonistic cooperation," [3] is a major
part of the pattern of restraint. The distribution of powers between
levels of government, for example, between the national and state
governments, is also an important restraint on government at the
various levels.

At this point we should take note of precisely what the Constitution has to say about the states. It establishes the relationship between the states and the national government, the federal relationship. Specifically, the Constitution lists delegated powers, those
which are specifically given to the national government. It also provides for other, so-called implied powers, necessary to carry out the
delegated ones. And the Tenth Amendment reads as follows: "The
powers not delegated to the United States by the Constitution, nor
prohibited to it by the states, are reserved to the states respectively,

---

[3] See Fred Krinsky and Gerald Rigby, *Theory and Practice of American
Democracy,* National, State, and Local Edition (Belmont, Calif.: Dickenson
Publishing Company, 1967), p. 201.

or to the people." Thus the Constitution establishes the relationship, or more precisely the basis of the relationship, of the two levels of government in the exercise of powers. It also lists, mainly in the amendments, a series of powers prohibited to the states. These provisions—for the delegated and implied powers of the central government, the reserved and prohibited powers of the states—set the framework for the relationship between the national government and the states that we call federalism, and we shall examine this relationship in detail shortly.

The Constitution also contains several provisions of guarantees or protections to the states. Article IV, Section 4, provides that "the United States shall guarantee to every state in this Union a republican form of government, and shall protect each of them against invasion; and on application of the legislature, or of the executive (when the legislature cannot be convened) against domestic violence." While it is by no means clear what "a republican form of government" is (inasmuch as the courts have consistently refused to define that term, declaring that it is a "political question" to be settled by the President and the Congress), it does seem possible to conclude that this provision makes the national government a protector of the states should their governing function be usurped. The requirement that it protect each state against invasion by another hardly seems necessary today, and invasion of any part of the United States by an external enemy instantly involves the whole country. As for the guarantee against domestic violence, it figured in several major cases in history, and recently, as a result of urban and racial unrest, it has again become a concern since federal assistance in handling riots and disturbances has been necessary. The final guarantees specified in the Constitution provide that no state shall be formed by joining two or more states or parts of states without the consent of the legislature of the states concerned, and that no state without its consent shall be deprived of its equal suffrage in the Senate. Although of historical importance, these would seem to be rather moot provisions in the last third of the twentieth century.

Perhaps the most important provision of the Constitution in relation to the states is the supremacy clause: "This Constitution, and the laws of the United States which shall be made in pursuance thereof; and all treaties made, or which shall be made, under the authority of the United States, shall be the supreme law of the land; and the judges in every state shall be bound thereby, anything in the Constitution or laws of any states to the contrary notwithstanding." This provision makes it perfectly clear that the relationship between the states and the national government is one in which there can be no conflict. Constitutionally there can be no conflict between valid national law and any state law. The conflict will be only apparent, for the supremacy clause clearly means that the national law will survive.

State Constitutions

State constitutions are popularly held in only slightly less reverence than the national Constitution. Constitutions, *per se*, are venerated; it would be political suicide to fail to make the proper incantations toward the holy writ of state politics. A student of our constitutional system, however, cannot accept ritualistic orthodoxy that does not conform with political reality.

Although it would be hazardous to disregard the status of the state constitution, such veneration underscores its real character—it is a political instrument. To fail to see it as a political document that defines the rules of the game, distributes privileges and protections, formalizes the relationships between various competitors for power, regulates the conditions under which they will compete and the techniques available to them, as well as specifying or at least predetermining the relative payoffs, will result in a failure to see the state constitution as an integral part of the political system.

It is useful to look at some illustrations that state constitutions provide of the privileges and special protection granted to certain groups and interests, which allow them to win more easily in the political process. Such illustrations can be found in almost every state constitution. Probably the most universal is the special protection and treatment for property holders and other taxpayers. Extensive provisions control legislative taxing powers, impose tax limits for local government, prohibit the states from borrowing money, and impose elaborate financial restraints on both state and local governments. Property tax exemptions are incorporated for religious groups and in many states for veterans. Bonuses, pensions, and advantages in the process of merit system selection are other examples of preferential treatment for veterans. Protestant-Catholic differences are reflected in state constitutional provisions concerning birth control and certain forms of gambling, such as bingo.

Almost every textbook on state and local government discusses deficiencies or shortcomings of state constitutions. While there is near unanimity on the need for thoroughgoing revision of state constitutions, some "deficiencies" are in fact the direct result of the growth of state constitutions as instruments of politics and may be rationally determined means of accomplishing an acceptable distribution of priv-

ileges and protections. As such they are not pathological to the system.
To establish a set of *a priori* assumptions about the "correct" nature of
the state constitution, its ingredients and provisions, and then to see
pathology because the provisions of the constitution do not coincide
with those assumptions, may lead to ill-advised prescriptions, which
may do great disservice to the "patient." [4] We do not pretend that
state constitutions are ideal, but we do insist upon a look at them
as they are *before* prescribing medication for a real or imagined
illness.

Most state constitutions fail to conform to the norm of a constitution: a set of fundamental principles, either unchanging or
changing gradually and definably, applicable to the past, present,
and future alike. Many of them are extremely long, and almost all
include detailed provisions dealing with statutory matters. Most are
frequently and easily amended. The most lengthy constitutions are
those of Louisiana, with approximately 210,000 words, Alabama with
80,000, and California with 75,000. At least 10 states have constitutions of 30,000 or more words, about three times as long as the
Constitution of the United States.

Length in itself is not a particularly difficult problem, but the kinds
of provisions that account for most of this length are. Examples include South Dakota's constitutional authorization for a twine and
cordage plant at the state penitentiary; Illinois' provision that
Chicago issue bonds to support the World Columbian Exposition,
held in 1893; until recent revision New York's constitution rendered
null and void all land grants made after 1775 by the King of England;
South Carolina's constitution defines a durable hard-surfaced street
in Greenville; and Louisiana's constitution, perhaps the worst of-
fender, includes 22 pages dealing with the rights of veterans and the
needy to receive pensions and other kinds of state aid. Other illustrations are manifold, but they serve only to demonstrate that state
constitutions almost universally incorporate excessively detailed provisions containing material that is rightfully statutory and should
be handled by the legislature, material that quickly becomes outdated, resulting in the need for frequent amendment.

A related criticism is frequency of amendment. Nine states have
amended their constitutions more than one hundred times. Louisiana
has enacted 439 amendments since 1921, and California is not far
behind with 350 changes since 1879. South Carolina has amended

---

[4] See Robert B. Dishman, *State Constitutions: The Shape of the Document*
(New York: National Municipal League, 1960) for a thorough consideration of
this topic.

its constitution 251 times, and Oregon, Alabama, Texas, New York, Florida, and Maryland have all done so between 100 and 250 times. A number of states have had several "fundamental laws"—Louisiana has had 10 constitutions, Georgia 8; Alabama, New York, and South Carolina 6; Arkansas, Florida, Texas, and Virginia, 5. Only 21 of the states are still operating under their original constitutions.[5]

Such lengthy, statutory, and frequently revised documents reflect a decided fear of legislative bodies, the extremes to which political interest groups have been able to incorporate their own vested interests into basic law, and the extent to which in many states the constitutional document fails to manifest real constitutionalism. The obsolescence of many of the provisions of these constitutions and their failure to form a basis for a governmental approach to the solution of current problems are the outstanding characteristics of state constitutions.

It would be incorrect, however, to suggest that all state constitutions are thus characterized. Many are viable manifestations of the fundamental pattern of governmental restraints. Our concern here for the "pathological" ingredients in some is to highlight the nature of constitutions and to suggest that an understanding of the political system of any given state requires an analysis of the character and role of that particular state's constitution. Our later consideration of the policymaking processes—the legislature, the executive, the judiciary, the party system, and the like—could not be meaningful unless we recognize that policymaking occurs under the general provisions of the state constitution. Insofar as the basic document makes temporary matters permanent, precludes flexibility and change (or is too easily changed in response to a momentarily dominant interest), entrenches special interests long past their time, or restrains the legislature in the approach to solutions of current problems, that document will seriously handicap the people of the state in the development of policy reflective of politically articulated demands.

Local Bases of Authority

The basic instrument of government for a local unit is the charter or a set of state laws (or even a single state law). The charter or state laws governing a local government, however, are not a constitution in the sense that the United States Constitution or the state constitutions are. The instrument is a grant by the state, either by

[5] For data on state constitutions see *The Book of the States* for the appropriate years, published by the Council of State Governments, Chicago.

state legislation or by the state constitution, which establishes the authority and responsibility of the local government, its legal powers and relationships. The pattern of restraints upon government at this level is imposed essentially by the provisions of the charter or set of state laws, and the nature of the charter or the laws cannot be understood apart from an understanding of the nature of the relationships between the state and its local units, the subject of Chapter 2.

2

Intergovernmental Relations
and the New Localism

The political system in the United States is a pattern of relationships of subsystems. To understand that pattern one must first understand the nature of a federal system generally and the way our federal system has developed specifically. Also important are the relationships between the state and local units and among the local units themselves, particularly within metropolitan areas.

Federalism in Theory and Practice

Federalism exists when there is a meaningful division of powers between two or more levels of government, so that each operates relatively independently of the other within its own sphere of powers. The exercise of powers is *relative*, and there is the possibility of change in the relationship of levels of government. At times one level may carry more or less weight than another in relation to a specific set of powers. Such elasticity has been one of the marked characteristics of our experience with federalism.

National and State Relations

The national government has specifically delegated powers, including the power to tax; borrow money; regulate interstate and foreign commerce; coin money and regulate its value; establish a postal system; create courts; declare war; maintain armies and a navy; assist the states in the maintenance of a militia; use the state militia to execute the laws of the land, suppress insurrections, and repel invasions; establish a uniform rule of naturalization; legislate on bankruptcies; fix standard weights and measures; punish counterfeiting; provide for patents and copyrights; define and punish piracies and felonies on the high seas and offenses against the law of nations; and govern the seat of the national government, the District of Columbia. These are powers granted by the Constitution.

No such list, however, could continue to be sufficient through all the changes of social, economic, and political conditions. Fortunately, the Constitution does not bind us to a static federalism. The national government is also authorized to "make all laws which shall be necessary and proper for carrying into execution the foregoing powers." This clause, variously referred to as the "necessary and proper" clause, the "implied powers" clause, or the "elastic" clause, makes the delegated powers pliable, capable of application to specific new problems that the government must face over the years.

Certain powers are specifically prohibited to government. For example, neither a state government nor the national government may pass a bill of attainder (a legislative imposition of punishment) or an ex post facto law, nor may they grant titles of nobility. The national government is specifically prohibited from suspending the writ of habeas corpus except in cases of rebellion or invasion or when the public safety may require it. It is also prohibited from imposing any direct tax except on the basis of population (modified by the Sixteenth Amendment), from imposing an export tax, or from giving any preference to the ports of one state over those of another. The states are specifically prohibited from entering into any treaty, coining money, passing any law impairing the obligation of contracts, or imposing duties on imports or exports without the consent of Congress.[1] All other powers—those not specifically delegated, implied, or prohibited—remain with the states or the people, as the Tenth Amendment reiterates.

This picture of the division of powers between the states and the national government is technically accurate but misleading. To emphasize the division of powers as an arbitrary system obscures the fact that there is more an interaction than a division of powers. The federal system is one of separate governments with interacting and complementary powers. The Constitution provides the basis for a meaningful division of powers between two levels of government, not a final specification of that division. Thus in American experience the problem of federalism has been and will continue to be the precise

---

[1] Article I, Sections 9 and 10. There are numerous other prohibitions on federal or state powers specifically written into the amendments, especially into the first eight and the fourteenth, and also interpreted into these amendments by the Supreme Court.

division of powers in a given case at a given time. It is just this relational aspect that is the key to the federal system. It is a system not so much of divided as shared powers, maximizing the opportunity of government at both levels to address problems and to attempt to solve them, but protected from disunity and potential internecine tendencies by the guarantee of supremacy of the government of the whole.

There are several provisions in the Constitution pertaining to the relationship between the national and state governments and among the states. The "full faith and credit" clause requires that each state recognize as valid all public acts, records, and judicial proceedings of every other state.[2] The "privileges and immunities" clause guarantees that every United States citizen will receive the privileges and immunities of his citizenship in any state he enters, thus preventing states from discriminating against nonresidents.[3] These two major clauses are important restraints on the states and have helped to establish a union of states rather than fifty independent ones.

Congress is prohibited from forming a state from the territory of another without its consent. The United States is obligated to guarantee to every state a republican form of government [4] and to protect the states against invasion and domestic violence upon their request.[5]

Contemporary political scientists describe this federal relationship between the states and the national government as a kind of "marble cake," as distinguished from a "layer cake," relationship, since the division of powers is not absolute.[6] Another popular way to describe this relationship is as "cooperative federalism," which suggests that each level of government approaches the solution of problems within its own sphere in a collaborative effort with one or more other levels of government.

State and Local Relationships

While the states existed before the federal union, and the national government was created through a specific act delegating powers, all local units—cities, counties, and special districts—are established by

---

[2] Criminal matters and divorce proceedings are notable exceptions.

[3] Important exceptions include the privilege of entering into certain professions and businesses—law, medicine, and barbering, for instance—and the use of the state's proprietary facilities—a state university, fish and game resources, and so on.

[4] See discussion in Chapter 1, p. 10.

[5] The President does not have to wait for such request if domestic violence interferes with the carrying out of federal statutes or federal court orders.

[6] The distinction is credited to Morton Grodzins, "The Federal System," in the American Assembly, *Goals for Americans,* edited by the President's Commission on National Goals (Englewood Cliffs, N.J.: Prentice-Hall, Inc., 1960).

and are subunits of the states. They have no inherent powers, and they are delegated no powers. They exercise only such powers as the state grants them, subject to its control.

The extent to which state controls are exercised, however, may vary. In most states such control is quite rigid. Notwithstanding provisions in most state constitutions prohibiting special legislation (legislative acts designed to apply to a specific city or local area and often discriminatory toward that area), some state legislatures sit as a kind of super city council. In others, various degrees of local self-government have been extended, ranging from fairly restrictive optional charter provisions (in which a city or county selects one of several proffered charters) to rather extensive home-rule provisions (in which the local community is free to govern itself within the organizational and functional areas specified). Yet even these relatively self-governing home-rule cities and counties receive permission for such government from the state by action of its legislature or provision of its constitution. With differing degrees of difficulty these provisions can be modified by the granting authority, and in most states judicial decisions have not been kind to those who advocate extensive home rule.[7] Thus home-rule cities or counties are independent of state interference primarily if and when it is convenient to the state for them to be so. They are not sovereign or independent in any sense comparable to the state in its relationship to the national government.

Cities are formed when in a limited geographic area there is a concentration of population and a need for solutions to problems incident to such concentration. Counties, on the other hand, are formed almost entirely as arbitrary lines drawn on a map sometime in a state's history. In most instances they represent convenient subdivisions for dispersing and carrying out state administrative activities. In most states counties have not been major governing units but rather administrative subunits (although there are notable exceptions, such as in California).

Special districts—governing units established to deal with one or a few functions—receive their authority from either general acts or special laws of the state legislature (usually the former). In both cases they are legally independent of existing governing units—state, city, and county—with their own powers and sources of revenue. They remain, however, legally subordinate to the state.

---

[7] An excellent source on home rule is Daniel R. Mandelker, *Managing Our Urban Environment* (Indianapolis, Ind.: Bobbs-Merrill Company, Inc., 1966), pp. 66–86.

While the United States Constitution does not mention local units, there has been a growing tendency for local governments to deal with the national government, sometimes even directly, particularly in the receipt of federal grants-in-aid. Local units have been drawn closer to the national government in mutual recognition of the need to solve the pressing problems of cities and metropolitan areas. Although we continue to adhere to the legal formality that the state is the parent and the local units the children, often the state is not an appropriate agency for solving the problems of local areas. These areas, particularly the metropolitan ones, increasingly are turning directly to the national government for assistance because the state is politically or financially incapable or unwilling to assume responsibility. Thus governmental relationships now involve not only a flexible federalism between state and national governments and a legal subordination of local to state government but also a new and increasingly direct relationship between national and local units.

The New Localism—Metropolitanism

The problem of relationships among local units has been magnified by the growth of metropolitanism. Currently, when one considers local government in the United States, a new social and economic entity, the metropolitan area, must be included. This entity has evolved in the last half century as the result of population trends in our society, particularly with respect to location.

There is one overriding demographic fact: the population of the United States is now predominantly urban. Over 70 percent of all Americans live in cities, and the decline in the rural population has become absolute as well as relative. No state is less than 35 percent urban, nearly half are more than 70 percent urban, and fewer than one-fifth are less than 50 percent urban.

A corollary to this increase is the growth of the suburbs surrounding the large central cities. In fact, almost all central cities have been growing, if at all, at a significantly slower pace than their adjoining suburbs. In the period from 1950 to 1960, central cities increased approximately 7 percent in population while the metropolitan suburbs grew by 50 percent. At the same time all but one (Los Angeles) of the 10 largest cities were losing population.

Approximately half of all the people living in metropolitan areas now reside outside the legal boundaries of the central cities. This is true of most of the large metropolitan areas, such as Boston, Philadelphia, St. Louis, Chicago, Los Angeles, and San Francisco.

The general population movement is not from rural areas to suburbs but primarily from rural and other urban but nonmetropolitan
areas to the metropolitan central cities, and from there to the suburbs.
While large numbers of people who seek jobs and services move to the
central cities, these same cities have been losing their more affluent
residents at an accelerating rate. Thus, the cities are left with an
increasingly large proportion of inhabitants in the lower income
brackets, demanding and needing additional public services, while
the more affluent, those able to own property and thus to support the
needed services through the property tax, are leaving the city for the
newer suburban areas. At the same time, the property tax base of
the central cities is diminishing as the physical property itself de-
teriorates through age and increasing neglect, thus producing a
smaller yield in taxes from which the rapidly accelerating demands
for services must be met.

Growth of Metropolitanism

The trend toward urban living is more correctly identified as the
growth of metropolitanism. Even though the Bureau of the Census'
definition has changed from time to time, a metropolitan area is
generally defined as the territory of a central city having at least
50,000 people and the county in which this city is situated, plus all
predominantly urban, contiguous counties. About two-thirds of the
people in the United States live in 230 metropolitan areas, and half of
the total population reside in the 15 largest ones. The number of
metropolises is increasing steadily, and the proportion of our population living in them promises to continue to increase. The metropolitan
population has been growing at a rate considerably more rapid than
that of the country as a whole. Not only is this an urban nation, it
is now distinctly a metropolitan nation.

But we are more than metropolitan; some metropolitan areas are
growing together to form "megalopolises" or supermetropolitan complexes, perhaps better designated as metropolitan regions.[8] The most
advanced of these regions extends over 600 miles down the eastern
coast from New Hampshire to Virginia, and includes parts of 10
states and 32 metropolitan areas. Within this vast urban region are
the metropolitan areas of Boston, New York, Philadelphia, Baltimore,
and Washington, D.C. Over 32,000,000 people—about 1 of every 6
people in the United States—live here. The region encompasses about

---

[8] The term "urban region" is seemingly attributable to Charlton F. Chute in
"Today's Urban Regions," *National Municipal Review* (June and July, 1956),
who defines it as two or more contiguous standard metropolitan areas.

one-fifth of the nation's retail store business and more than one-fifth of the nation's manufacturing activity. Across the continent on the west coast, the Los Angeles area is fast combining with metropolitan San Diego over 100 miles south, and three contiguous metropolitan areas (comprising most of Los Angeles, Orange, and San Bernardino counties) include nearly 50 percent of the population of California. This urban region includes 10 million people, 7½ million of whom live in the Los Angeles area. Projections suggest that 20 million people will live in this region by the end of the century. Some metropolitan regions, and many metropolitan areas, spill across the boundaries of two or more states, and four intrude into other countries.[9]

These population trends—movement to the central cities, growth of the suburbs, and development of metropolitan areas and regions— are of prime importance in the political and economic life of this country today. No other single phenomenon is as critical to an understanding of what is happening in the United States. For example, during the last 10 years the metropolitan areas have accounted for between 70 and 80 percent of the nation's economic value added by manufacture, of manufacturing establishments, of total industrial employment, of all manufacturing payrolls, of all bank deposits, and of all housing starts.[10] Likewise urban demands, interests, and political power are the stuff of politics and the major domestic concern of government. The politically important questions of today are increasingly defined by the two-thirds of the population living in urban and metropolitan areas.

The political power of cities is increased by the fact that metropolitan complexes tend to be located in the highly populated states, making the city vote crucial in the accumulation of electoral votes in a presidential election. The creation in 1965 of the Department of Housing and Urban Development underscores the fact of urban political power. Furthermore, the mandatory reapportionment of state legislative districts, which has come about as a result of several decisions by the Supreme Court,[11] has changed the relative strength

[9] Detroit, Michigan-Windsor, Canada; San Diego, California-Tijuana, Mexico; El Paso, Texas-Cuidad Juarez, Mexico; and Laredo, Texas-Nuevo Laredo, Mexico.

[10] Advisory Commission on Intergovernmental Relations, *Alternative Approaches to Governmental Reorganization in Metropolitan Areas* (Washington, D.C.: U.S. Government Printing Office, 1962), p. 5.

[11] The two best sources on reapportionment are Howard D. Hamilton (ed.), *Legislative Apportionment: Key to Power* (New York: Harper and Row, Publishers, 1964), an anthology of readings and sources on state legislative apportionment; and Glendon Schubert, *Reapportionment* (New York: Charles Scribner's Sons, 1965), a thorough research anthology, including articles and sources covering every aspect of reapportionment.

of the cities and rural areas in state legislatures, with predictable political consequences. In California, for instance, a reapportionment act adopted in 1965 inclined the balance of representation in the state legislature toward metropolitan Southern California, giving Los Angeles County (only part of the Southern California metropolitan region) 14½ instead of 1 senator. Eight Southern California counties now have 46 of the 80 lower house (Assembly) seats and 22 of the 40 Senate seats. The competition for political power will be increasingly competition for support of the city and the urban region. Thus the problems of governing a metropolitan society will dominate the domestic concerns of government at all levels.

Disparity of Jurisdiction and Problem Area

The development of an urban-metropolitan society has great importance for local government. Most important domestic problems facing the United States involve the large metropolitan areas, yet governmental jurisdiction is still defined largely as it was 150 years ago. As a result, in most states our twentieth-century society is being governed with eighteenth-century arrangements.

In most states a city ordinarily cannot operate beyond the limits of its own legally defined boundaries. Yet obviously problems do not respect city boundary lines. Pressing social problems—crime, health, public welfare, slums, air pollution, sewage disposal, water supply, transportation—cannot usually be either defined or solved within the jurisdictional boundaries of existing cities. They are area-wide problems and require area-wide solutions. Furthermore, many metropolitan problems spread across state and even international lines. Thus not only are there metropolitan problems without metropolitan-wide machinery for generating solutions but also those that fall within the gray zone between state authority and federal jurisdiction and, in the case of international lines, the even darker zone of international jurisdictions.

Fragmentation and Multiplicity of Governments

Recognizing the disparity between jurisdiction and problem area, most states have created additional units and levels of government in a random effort to cope with specific problems. Consequently, local government is at present characterized by a multiplicity of governing units and a fragmentation of governmental responsibility. In 1967 the 230 metropolitan areas contained more than 20,000 separate governmental units. Chicago, at the extreme, listed 1,113 units of local government in its metropolitan area. It is not unusual for such an area to include part of two states, two or more counties, scores of cities, and hundreds of special districts.

Counties have not proved effective in governing or administering the larger areas, for they are, on the whole, the most antiquated and archaic of American governing institutions.[12] They almost always lack an effective executive, being governed by collegial bodies. Although it has not been established conclusively that counties cannot be modified so as to become effective units, the fact is that there have been few attempts to do so.[13] They are basically rural administrative agencies and agents of the state, generally unsuited to the demands of a metropolitan age.

Special districts are a popular means of overcoming the rigidity of the boundary lines of general local units and their consequent inability to attack area-wide problems.[14] There are special districts for almost every conceivable purpose, the most popular being schools but also including street lighting, fire protection, irrigation, air pollution control, transportation, and cemetery maintenance. These districts are superimposed upon existing governmental structures, and the jurisdiction of a given special district may extend, for example, over more than one municipality, over both city and county territory, or may be limited to a small part of a municipality or unincorporated territory. Special districts may, and frequently do, overlap each other, so that a resident of a given city may be subject to the governmental authority not only of a municipality but also of the county, a school district, and several other special-purpose districts.

The reasons for this hodgepodge of governing units are not hard to identify. The most important has already been mentioned—the inappropriateness of the traditional structure for the solution of problems that cannot be contained within the jurisdictional boundaries of the existing governing units. Often the local government simply does not have the legal authority to tackle a specific problem, such as air pollution, or the problem may be such that the exercise of authority by the existing units is largely ineffective, as in the case of widespread crime.

---

[12] Not all students of local government agree, however. See, for instance, George S. Blair, *American Local Government* (New York: Harper and Row, Publishers, 1964), especially pp. 193–95, in which the trends in county government are read to suggest a considerably brighter picture.

[13] The most encouraging modification to provide an effective executive at this governmental level has been the institution of a county manager, chief administrative officer, or elected chief executive. However, only a relatively small number of counties have adopted any of these plans.

[14] The leading study of special districts is John C. Bollens, *Special District Governments in the United States* (Berkeley: University of California Press, 1957).

Sometimes existing governments have inadequate financial resources, for most cities have rigid limits on their power to tax and borrow, limits imposed upon them by the state legislature or the state constitution. Sometimes, as in the case of school districts, the rationale for creating a special district is to free the activity from the actual or potential control of the city government. Whatever the reasons for creating new units of government, the results usually involve a less than adequate overall accomplishment of major governmental services, considerable duplication and overlapping, unevenness and gaps in services, multiple levels of taxation, and confusion of the citizenry as to who is responsible. In fact, many citizens are not even aware of the existence of the multiple levels of government to which they are presumably responsible and which they presumably control.

Problems of the Central City

The continued growth of cities and metropolitan areas has posed special problems for the major cities. We have already noted the impact of the direction of population movement in replacing the more affluent members of the central city with the more needy. As the central city has grown older it has grown poorer, with a higher concentration of the underprivileged. The combination of an increasing demand for services and diminishing property values seriously affects its abilities to furnish such services. The vicious circle is perpetuated since deteriorating property requires higher property taxes in order to produce the same amount of revenue, increased needs require additional revenue (not to mention the impact of inflationary tendencies), with the result that both affluent residents and taxpaying businesses and industries flee to the suburbs, which are both physically and financially more attractive.

One of the more serious problems facing the central city is the provision of services for those who no longer reside or never have resided there, who live in the suburban fringe and are employed within the central city. Although much of the cost of such services is borne by the businesses employing them through taxes paid to the city, the mere increase in the central city's daytime population caused by these commuters places a severe burden on it. It must provide the services demanded for those who live there and for the suburbanites, but the latter, except in a few exceptional cases, are taxed little or nothing to pay for the services. A special problem for the central city is the need for extensive transportation and parking facilities. Many major cities now devote almost 50 percent of their downtown areas to moving and parking cars. In our modern metropolises much of the high-speed highway system, as well as most of the parking facilities, are required not only for residents of the city but also for suburban commuters.

Of course, this daytime influx of people is essential, and some economic benefits do accrue to the central city, but the drain on its financial resources and the challenge to its service-providing agencies are often more than it can stand. A few cities have imposed a tax on payrolls or income derived from employment within the city regardless of place of residence. The evidence is inconclusive as to whether this will help solve the problems faced by the central city, but the gravity of the problem is underscored by the adoption of such measures.

The physical deterioration of the major cities is widespread and obvious. Much of their property, both residential and industrial, is either physically deteriorating, functionally obsolete, or both. Once-great residential areas have been reduced to multifamily apartment districts. Massive parts of the central cities have become slums. We have noted that people who can afford to are leaving the cities in increasing numbers, being replaced by those of less affluence, which brings about further physical deterioration of property, and new industries increasingly seek the suburbs or specifically industrial towns away from the central city. The results are inevitable: greater deterioration of the existing property and the infectious spread of blight and its accompanying social and economic costs—increasing crime, diminishing health, accentuated educational demands, and the shrinking availability of cultural and recreational facilities.

Less easily demonstrated but far more serious are the effects on people. Many who remain in the central city reflect an inheritance of deprivation. As Daniel Mandelker put it, the central city has become "an institutional caretaker for the deprived and the underprivileged." [15] The evidence is accumulating that an increasing number of American people in our central cities are frustrated by the great American dream and are convinced that the promises it holds are illusionary, that life can be no better.[16]

Prominent among the by-products of decay is the social trauma of the central city. Its changing complexion and the wide disparity between its social composition and that of suburban communities pose serious problems that at least partly explain the increasing inci-

[15] Mandelker, op. cit., p. 6.
[16] Among those who address themselves to the character of urban life should be listed primarily Eric Fromm, Escape From Freedom (New York: Holt, Rinehart & Winston, Inc., 1941), and David Riesman, The Lonely Crowd (New Haven, Conn.: Yale University Press, 1950).

dence of violence and social disruption. The most striking difference between suburban areas and central cities is racial; the latter are becoming places to live for nonwhite people. Each succeeding census, for example, demonstrates that the concentration of the Negro in the central cities continues to increase. Many cities doubled their Negro population in the last 10 years, and Negro birth rates are increasing disproportionately to the Negro population. Washington, D.C. is now more than 55 percent Negro, and two of every three births there is to a Negro family.

Along with this high concentration of nonwhites, though no causal relationship is implied, are lower per capita incomes, more broken homes, higher unemployment rates, lower educational levels, increased crime, and greater demands on education. (This catalog suggests the real cost of 100 years of neglect of the Negro and other nonwhite groups.) Such social costs, disturbing in themselves and frightening in their implications, are what our society must face in the age of metropolitanism. Can the central city, developed in a premetropolitan era, operating with governing instruments appropriate to the nineteenth century, unadapted and in many cases unadaptable to present and future requirements meet the challenges of today and tomorrow?

Governing the Metropolis

It is easier to define the problems than to devise the solutions. The difficulties resulting from the growth of metropolises suggest the need, however, for serious consideration of alternative means to govern them, or at least for evaluation of current institutions and presently used techniques.

Proposals for metropolitan reorganization, for the creation of new means of governing metropolitan areas, have been numerous, but their implementation has been infrequent. The impediments to such proposals are impressive. We have already seen that constitutions often provide in detail for the organization and powers of local governments, and they may have so entrenched certain interests that a modification of local government would require major overhauling of the established distribution of power and privilege, a task not easily accomplished. Furthermore, the legal relationship between the state and the local communities usually requires that any such attempts be made by the state legislature, by the electorate through amendment of the constitution or by both. Further handicapping those who would make changes is the inertia surrounding well-established governing arrangements, a reluctance to tinker with familiar ways of doing things.

Apparently the most serious impediment to any major change is the strong "grass roots" tradition, which holds that democracy works best "close to the people" and that local government is the backbone of democratic government. Modifications that either actually or seemingly involve any movement away from local control, from close connection between the people and their local institutions, run afoul of this notion. (See Chapter 4 for further consideration of the role and significance of the traditional grass roots democracy.) Any suggestions for change at the local level must fight an uphill battle for acceptance in a society which historically has emphasized the virtues of government at the local level.

Nevertheless, numerous suggestions have been made, and a few have been tried. A new kind of reform movement for local government has arisen, differing significantly in its basic purposes and radically in its proffered solutions from the older one. The chief intention of the older reform movement, dating from about the turn of the present century, was to rid the cities of the evils of political corruption. Its basic assumptions were (1) politics and politicians are at best necessary evils, not to be trusted and not genuinely identified with the public good, and (2) good government could best be attained through application of business principles. The slogan, "Economy, Efficiency, and Morality," sums up the general concerns of this movement.

One of the identifying features of the earlier reformers was their concern for new structural arrangements. For instance, their efforts to rid the city of strong political bosses led to the substitution of new forms of city government, such as the commission and council-manager forms. Notwithstanding their very different aims and suggested solutions, their concern for institutional change and tendency to emphasize structure and form as the areas in which change is most needed links them rather closely with the present-day reformer now concentrating on the need for restructuring the government of the metropolitan area.

Suggestions for metropolitan reform have largely emphasized consolidation toward area-wide metropolitan government. Numerous approaches have been proposed. We will consider them in order, from those requiring little or no modification of existing institutions to those calling for elaborate structural changes.

Extraterritorial Powers

The most obvious difficulty that often arises as a result of rigidly defined governmental jurisdictions is the inability to provide services to those in need simply because they are beyond the territorial limits of the unit able to furnish the service. People are apt to be more aware of this problem when it involves services such as fire protection, ambulances, or buses than when it involves more significant but less-easily identified problems such as protection against disease, control of crime, and the location of sewage disposal plants. Sometimes municipalities are granted the power to extend their jurisdiction beyond their territorial limits to supply certain services or to meet certain specific needs. In some states the courts have upheld this extraterritorial jurisdiction as essential to carrying out powers specifically granted to the city. While this is a useful technique to respond to a specific need, it does not constitute a permanent solution to the basic problem because it represents a piecemeal approach. The necessary coordination and integration of services required for overall effective solution of the problems confronting a metropolis are lacking. Furthermore, the problems of financing and location of responsibility (since extraterritoriality means extension of governing powers over people who have no role in the selection and control of the government exercising those powers) constitute serious limitations. Most important, however, is the possibility that such piecemeal solutions may often hide the real need for more general solutions and that the apparent benefit derived may eliminate political pressure for more appropriate changes.

Intergovernmental Cooperation

The most widely used means to coordinate activities of governments in the metropolitan area involves informal cooperation or, sometimes, formal contractual relationships. Such arrangements are usually limited to the provision of services, such as fire protection, police, water, and health, and exclude matters involving regulation or control. The most formalized technique for intergovernmental cooperation is the Lakewood Plan, so named because it was first used by the city of Lakewood in Los Angeles County. Under this plan a municipality that cannot or does not wish to provide certain services itself, will contract with the county government for these services. Thus a city may contract for police protection and for engineering and planning work, indeed for almost any basic municipal activity. This plan has been most widely used in Los Angeles County, where dozens of cities retain autonomy but provide virtually no services for themselves, contracting for them with the county. While obviously extremely useful in solving some problems of individual cities, this technique is not a solution to the general problems of a metropolitan area.

Functional Consolidation

Functional consolidation is the merging of a single function performed by two or more units of government into a single agency belonging to one government, which then provides the service. Such an arrangement requires no major changes in structure beyond those involved with the specific function, and thus is generally more acceptable than more radical renovation. On the other hand, it is again obvious that functional consolidation, while it may be an adequate solution for providing particular services, is not a general solution to the complex problems of the metropolitan area.

Metropolitan Special District

The creation of metropolitan special districts has been looked upon with some favor for a number of years. Under this arrangement, area-wide problems can be turned over to a special district without substantially interfering with already established political and structural arrangements. However, the metropolitan special district involves the same disadvantages and problems of special districts *per se*. While some state legislatures have been willing to allow such special districts to become multipurpose units, incorporating into their jurisdiction several troublesome problems, local communities have generally been reluctant to transfer functions to them. Metropolitan districts, some dating back over half a century, therefore remain essentially single-purpose governments.

Apparently the oldest are the Chicago Sanitary District, set up in 1889, and the Massachusetts Metropolitan District, which became responsible for sewers in 1889, parks in 1893, and water in 1895. In more recent years Louisville has set up a metropolitan sewer district, the Port of New York Authority has been created to provide transportation services, and the St. Louis area has formed a bi-state development agency. One of the most potentially extensive of these special districts is the Municipality of Metropolitan Seattle, set up in 1958. However, so far its services are limited to sewage disposal. Some proponents of the metropolitan district argue that it is a first step toward eventual amalgamation of various local units, but the record suggests this does not happen rapidly, if at all.

Annexation

The oldest and most familiar procedure for coordinating the activities of central cities and their surrounding territory has been annexation to the central city. While this familiar technique has been used extensively, it is not easily accomplished when the city is surrounded by suburban municipalities. Opposition in suburban areas is often vehement, based on some facts and a great deal of speculation that taxes would be higher and services slower, that the central city is corrupt, that the suburban areas would have to subsidize the rebuilding of a largely blighted central city, and that local autonomy and democracy would be diminished. Although it is highly doubtful that all of these are realistic bases for opposition, it can safely be said that the political climate for large-scale annexation in a metropolitan area is simply nonexistent. This technique is and may continue to be a useful tool for consolidating unincorporated territory into cities, but it promises little as a solution to the problems of governing metropolitan areas.

Metropolitan Federation

One of the most widely known methods of reorganization is the metropolitan federation, patterned roughly after the American federal experience. The division of powers is between a central metropolitan government, sometimes the county, and the preexisting units of local government, primarily municipalities. The metropolitan government exercises those powers essential to providing solutions to metropolitan-wide problems, while the local units retain powers related specifically to local matters. The analogy is attractive, and the traditional appeal of federalism is such as to make this proposal initially inviting even to some who are otherwise not disposed toward metropolitan government. The difficulties are obvious, however, for dividing powers between local and metropolitan governments is not an easy task even on paper, not to mention the difficulties that come to mind if the division were to be attempted in an operating political arena. In principle, such division might be possible; in practice, it is very likely to be impossible.

The most successful example of this kind of arrangement is the Toronto, Canada area. The Municipality of Metropolitan Toronto, federated in 1953, was created by the provincial parliament and given jurisdiction over metropolitan functions, while the City of Toronto and its twelve suburban neighbors retained responsibility for local matters. The new metropolitan government is responsible for such things as water supply, sewage disposal, housing, education, interurban highways, parks, and planning. Initially, the cities were left in charge of police, fire, health, library, and most welfare services. In 1957 law enforcement became a metropolitan responsibility.

The most recent federation developed in Miami and Dade County,

Florida. In 1957 the Dade County metropolitan district was adopted, with a reorganized county government becoming the area-wide unit and 26 cities being retained for local activities. The first ten years of this federation were tumultuous, and what the future holds for it remains to be seen.

City-County Consolidation and Separation

Some advocates of metropolitan reform have proposed either city-county consolidation or separation. Under the former, which has been adopted in Philadelphia, New York, Baton Rouge, and Nashville, the city limits are extended to coincide with the county covering the metropolitan region. Although the particular arrangements vary, the essential idea is to have the city and the county governments coincide, forming one overall governing unit for the metropolitan area. Such a proposal is difficult to effect when there are other existing municipalities in the metropolitan areas, as well as when the metropolitan area does not neatly coincide with the geographic limits of the county. However, the advocates of this kind of change are encouraged by the continued, though sporadic, interest in and occasional adoption of consolidation.

City-county separation is essentially the reverse of consolidation; the city is divorced from the county in which it has been located, eliminating at least one government under which residents live. The most important examples of this process are Baltimore, separated from its county in 1851, San Francisco, in 1856, St. Louis, in 1875, and Denver, in 1903. Such separation is scarcely a solution for today's metropolitan problems.

Metropolitan Reform in Review

This catalog of proposed metropolitan reform is of necessity incomplete. Some people support modifications other than the ones suggested, and combinations of the ones here included are pet projects of others. Nevertheless, the major reforms that have been tried or widely advocated have been presented, and the brief review given is sufficient to suggest several general conclusions of more importance to the student of local government than the particular ingredients of a specific proposal.

First, it is fairly clear that it is impossible to effect the more radical plans where their proponents think them necessary, and where they are possible they are not necessary. In other words, where there is enough cooperation among units of government in the metropolis and sufficient absence of hostile groups to make the adoption of a comprehensive proposal such as federation possible, that proposal is not necessary to solve the problems facing the metropolitan area since most of those problems can be worked out through extensive cooperative efforts.

Second, most proposal place far too much emphasis upon structure and form and too little on the realities of the distribution of political power in the metropolitan area. No structural change can be successful unless it is based on a realistic appraisal of the demands of the communities in which it is to be instituted. Yet most of the proposals reflect a dedication, usually unarticulated, to the notion that if we could just find the proper arrangement of governmental institutions the results would be favorable.

Third, the tradition of localism and the idea of grass-roots democracy are very strong, and any attempts to solve the problems of the metropolis that counter those traditions stand little chance of adoption and less chance of success, even if they were adopted. The opposition here is strong and vehement, and a simple awareness of the complexity of the problem and the urgency for improvement will not suffice to overcome it. Any proposals, any changes that are to have a real chance for success must take into account these traditions and the strength of the opposition to increasing the size of government.

Fourth, proposals for modifying the government in metropolitan areas must take into account political realities in the communities involved. It is not a matter of designing the best plan or of finding the most expert way of establishing an efficient and economic governmental structure. The problem is to work out through political processes the most acceptable solutions, maximizing the value of the expert within the realities of the political dimension. As Daniel Grant notes:

After running the gamut of pros and cons of annexation, contractual arrangements, extraterritorial powers, special districts, the federated metropolis, and city consolidation or separation, virtually all of the studies conclude with the same pessimistic note—those "solutions" which are adequate are not politically feasible and those which are politically feasible are not adequate.[17]

While concern for structural arrangements is necessary, many people fail to recognize that forms of government are not solutions in themselves but only means toward solutions. An affection for a particular institutional arrangement must not lead one into the error

[17] Daniel R. Grant, "Federal-Municipal Relationships and Metropolitan Integration," *Public Administration Review,* XIV (Autumn, 1954), 259.

of assuming that adopting this specific structure will guarantee success in solving problems. However, careful consideration of alternative arrangements may indicate that some can be expected to hinder while others promote satisfactory solution of problems. But whatever the efforts toward solution, they will both determine and be determined by the political ingredient in the affected area. It is to the political ingredient that we turn in Chapter 3.

3

The Theoretical Framework for Politics

In the United States all politics is ultimately local. There is no
national politics, and political parties are not national parties. After
their periodic cooperative efforts to win national elections, parties
tend to devolve into their independent and widely varying units.
These units usually are not even state parties. The only significant
on-going political involvement is at the local level—county, city, and
precinct.

This political particularism justifies considering politics at the
local level, but understanding local politics requires explaining the
nature of the democratic political process in general and the role of
elections, the electorate, political parties, and political interest groups
specifically. In the present chapter these theoretical concerns [1] will
be considered as a framework for later discussion of the institutional
and procedural aspects of politics at the state and local levels.

The Nature of the Democratic Political Process

Probably the most difficult task in any political system is to solve
the problem of the legitimacy of political power. How to decide who
governs and how to transfer power in an orderly and politically acceptable fashion are central problems that distinguish democratic
from nondemocratic systems.

The democratic political process may be described as an open com-

---

[1] Much of the analysis in this chapter is drawn from Fred Krinsky and
Gerald Rigby, *Theory and Practice of American Democracy*, National, State,
and Local Edition (Belmont, Calif.: Dickenson Publishing Company, 1967),
by permission of the authors and publisher.

petition for political power. The locus of political power is not easily identified, and the wielders of power—those who make public policy—are numerous. Normally, however, those who make public policy are privileged to do so because they have won the struggle against others who sought the same privilege.

The distinguishing characteristic of American politics is this open competition for power. The crucial question is not who governs but how those in power get there. It is not by virtue of inheritance, physical force, superior economic standing, membership in an elite group, or any process other than open competition for the approval of the people, although some or all of these factors may weigh heavily in the competitive process. This does not mean, of course, that all policymakers are personally involved in elections, for many are in fact appointed. Nevertheless, their appointments are a result of the open competition engaged in by those who appoint them. That is, it is the winners of the competition who are privileged to fill the great number of appointive offices.[2]

There is no conflict between this analysis of the nature of the democratic process and the argument of classic democratic theorists about the sovereign people as the source of government and the grantors of power. As long as political power depends upon victory in an open competition in which the people make the final choice, political power is dependent upon those people, and governors become governors by their action. The basis for the people's participation in the governing process is this competition, and power flows to those who win the votes of the electorate.[3]

This analysis of the nature of the American political process assumes certain prerequisites. Democratic politics requires, first, a regularized procedure for an effective periodic transfer of power, a procedure for the participation of the electorate as the final determiners of who is victorious. This procedure must reflect a verifiable expectation on the part of the people that they can periodically transfer power from one set of officials to another. "Paper" provisions will not suffice; experience must show that those in power get there and

[2] To the extent that civil service fills appointive positions without regard to who wins, the political victor is not able to shape that system, but it is well established in theory and practice that the civil service employees are responsible to the elected representative and therefore obliged to function according to his wishes.

[3] "*The people are powerless if the political enterprise is not competitive.* It is the competition of political organizations that provides the people with the opportunity to make a choice. Without this opportunity popular sovereignty amounts to nothing." E. E. Schattschneider, *The Semisovereign People* (New York: Holt, Rinehart & Winston, Inc., 1960), p. 140.

stay there as a result of an open competition for the favor of the people. Some type of election, then, is assumed. And this election must be a meaningful way for the people to replace those who govern. It must be the final stage of an open competition in which the people can genuinely choose who will be allowed to govern.

A second prerequisite in the political process is unrestricted participation. The process of competition is institutionalized, that is, the ability to compete is protected by guarantees so that all who wish to compete may do so with a meaningful chance to win. Ideally, no potential competitor will be told before the competition that he is not allowed to compete. We have not attained the ideal, however. Excluding Negroes from registering or voting, prohibiting Communists from appearing on the ballot, and setting property or literacy qualifications for voting are all prior restraints on the openness of participation. Regardless of the justifications suggested for such restrictions, they nevertheless qualify the unrestricted participation presumed in a democratic political process. Obviously, the corollary of unrestricted participation is freedom to organize, criticize, and differ, for these are indispensable ingredients in any genuinely competitive process. Competition cannot be meaningful unless it is based on freedom of speech and action.

A third presumption of the democratic political process is the acquiescence of the losers. Once the electorate has spoken and a winner has emerged, those who did not win accept their defeat and allow the winners to govern. There is no revolution, suspension of the constitution, assassination of the opponent, or withdrawal from the political arena. Those who do not gain office, furthermore, are not really losers, for all they have lost is the momentary grasp of power. This is never a final defeat, and the temporary losers are institutionally guaranteed the privilege, and indeed have the responsibility, of continuing to compete for power. They cannot and may not prevent the winners from governing, but they are privileged to continue to oppose, both within and without the government, to campaign, educate, criticize, propose alternative policies, and to stand ready to challenge the incumbents in their formation and implementation of policy.

The Role of Elections and the Electorate

Many textbooks on state and local government examine in detail the structure of political parties, the intricacies of elections and electoral law, and the minutiae of voting procedures without insuring that the reader has a basic understanding of the role of elections and of the electorate in the democratic process. Here the assumption is that knowledge of the details of the electoral process is virtually useless without a clear understanding of the meaning of that process and why rules and procedures exist at all.

Traditional democratic theory has not helped a great deal in understanding the role of elections and the electorate, for it has regarded elections as the way the "general will" could be expressed on major policy questions. This is the way our electoral process is explained in far too many instances, but it is not an accurate portrayal of reality. Policymaking by the electorate is not the rationale for elections. Elections cannot accomplish this goal, and the electorate is not equipped to function in this fashion. Criticism of this traditional view has grown as contrary empirical evidence has become more persuasive.[4]

Elections—national, state, or local—serve as an integral part of the competition for political power. Their primary function is to allow the voters to participate in the competitive struggle. The election is the culmination of a concentrated campaign, the most public and open phase of the continuing competition for power. Elections do not decide what government shall do but who will preside over the process of deciding what government shall do.

Elections, of course, have serious implications for public policy. Who wins will obviously affect the kind of policy developed. Yet the difference between the winners and losers is seldom great enough to distinguish clear alternatives that might have occurred had the other competitors won. The election demands that the competitors appeal to a broad cross section of society in the interest of maximizing their votes, with the result that the election seldom if ever clearly indicates

[4] Early evidence of this criticism is the following statement by Joseph A. Schumpeter more than a quarter of a century ago: "Our chief troubles about the classical theory centered in the proposition that 'the people' hold a definite and rational opinion about every individual question and that they give effect to this opinion—in a democracy—by choosing 'representatives' who will see to it that that opinion is carried out. Thus the selection of the representatives is made secondary to the primary purpose of the democratic arrangement which is to vest the power of deciding political issues in the electorate. Suppose we reverse the roles of these two elements and make the deciding of issues by the electorate secondary to the election of the men who are to do the deciding. . . . We now take the view that the role of the people is to produce a government, or else an intermediate body which in turn will produce a national executive or government. And we define: the democratic method is that institutional arrangement for arriving at political decisions in which individuals acquire the power to decide by means of a competitive struggle for the people's vote." *Capitalism, Socialism, and Democracy* (New York: Harper and Row, Publishers, 1942), p. 269.

critical differences in program orientation. Explanations of the results of an election as a mandate for a particular policy or a series of policy decisions may be a useful technique in politics, but it is less than precise as an analytical statement. Elections do not produce mandates; they produce governors. Serious competitors for political power, at all levels, knowing that they must maximize their vote in an election, do not ordinarily deviate far from the well-recognized mean in terms of policy, since such appeals would not likely win an election. In this sense, the necessity of competing for the electorate's vote does set the outer limits of policy proposals.

Angus Campbell has reviewed the evidence for the adequacy of normative democratic theory on the functioning of elections. A brief summary of that discussion is pertinent here.[5] Campbell suggested that normative democratic theory generally assumes two facts about the role of the election as a means by which the acts of government can be brought under the control of the governed. First, it assumes that the public is aware of goals and has the ability to decide which policies can best attain such goals. Second, the election is assumed to present the voters with recognizable policy alternatives which have attracted partisan commitment in such a way that the electorate can make a definite choice between them.

Campbell observed that there is much evidence that the electorate lacks an awareness of policy. Individually, the voter does not know the issues, does not understand the alternatives, and generally, when aware, is oriented only to the general problem, not its specifics or the implications of the policy. Collectively, the electorate displays no coherent pattern of beliefs relative to policy on major questions such as welfare legislation, foreign affairs, the economy, or civil liberties. There is scant evidence of ideological commitment, only programmatic preferences. Furthermore, little evidence exists that the electorate is certain what specific policies one party or the other would carry out; that is, party alternatives in terms of policy alternatives are not generally recognized.

This gives us a portrait of the electorate as almost wholly without any detailed information about decisionmaking in government, knowing little about what government has done because of previous elections or what government will do as a result of the present election, and unable to appraise its goals or the appropriateness of the means chosen to meet them. As a result, the electoral decision will be ambig-

[5] See Angus Campbell, *The American Voter* (New York: John Wiley & Sons, Inc., 1960), pp. 541–48. Also available by the same publisher is an abridged form in paperback published in 1964; see pp. 280–85.

uous as to specific government acts and will give to those who frame policy real freedom. Elections will bring little pressure from the electorate on the policymakers; such pressure almost always comes from groups with specific interests, not from the body politic.

What, then, is the importance of elections with respect to policy? The election defines broad goals and the very generalized means of reaching them, not specific goals and means. The electoral decision expresses the comparison of total images of one party with that of the other, and these images reflect certain differences of generalized goals and means. Hence, the electoral process sets the bounds of an acceptable policy discussion; it limits the appeal to be made in the competition. This does not suggest that the electorate is insignificant nor that its decisions are unimportant. Indeed, this limited but realistic role of the electorate marks the significant difference between our political scheme and those where the electoral decision is manipulated and the competition for votes is not genuinely open.

Morris Janowitz and Dwaine Marvick investigated the prerequisites for a democratic election, one that reflects a "process of consent" rather than a "process of manipulation." [6] They suggest three requirements. First, a democratic election requires a competition between opposing candidates that pervades the entire constituency. Second, both parties must engage in efforts to maintain established voting blocs, to recruit independent voters, and to gain converts from the opposite party. Third, both parties must vigorously attempt to win the current election and attempt long-run advancement of their chances to succeed in later elections.

Janowitz and Marvick suggest that five elements must be present for the competition to make for consent rather than manipulation of the electorate. First, the election must produce high levels of participation among all groups of citizens. Second, participation must be based upon political self-confidence as well as self-interest. Third, the competition must stimulate effective political deliberation as a basis for the electoral decision. Fourth, there must be no monopoly of the mass media. Fifth, interpersonal pressures must operate independently of the influence of the mass media. If these criteria are met, elections will be genuinely competitive, and the electorate can perform its primary function of selecting governors.

These elements of competition suggest that while the basic purpose

[6] See Morris Janowitz and Dwaine Marvick, *Competitive Pressure and Democratic Consent* (Ann Arbor, Mich.: University of Michigan, 1956). A summary is reprinted in Heinz Eulau, Samuel J. Eldersveld, and Morris Janowitz, *Political Behavior: A Reader in Theory and Research* (New York: The Free Press, 1956), pp. 275–86.

of an election is to enable the electorate to determine who wins, the process of competition may involve some degree of manipulation. The less manipulative the election, that is, the more sophisticated the tools of competition, the more desirable the outcome of the election is apt to be. Nonetheless, in any given election all the electorate can do is to choose between the alternatives presented to it by the competitors. In the long run, the alternative candidates or programs presented to the electorate will reflect its level of sophistication. Each party will tend to compete for the electorate's vote at the level necessary to maximize support of its candidates. If one competitor more accurately calculates the appropriate kind of appeal, he will win the election.

Traditional democratic theory has set up requirements for the components of electoral decisions and the characteristics of the electorate.[7] For instance, it has been assumed that the electoral decision must be the result of full information and knowledge on the part of the voters and that they must possess political principle or moral standards. Furthermore, the electorate is required to observe and perceive political reality accurately, to be able to communicate and discuss, and to reflect rational judgment in political decision. Finally, the voters are supposed to react in consideration of the common good or community interest rather than in self-interest.

These normative requirements for the electorate, however, are not necessary to the operation of a competitive electoral process. Electorate knowledge, principle, rationality, involvement, and interest may make the competitors raise more significant questions. But the crucial factor is still whether those who govern are privileged to do so as a result of getting the vote of the people, even though those people may not meet the norm required by traditional democratic theory.

This is an important point. What a democratic society must promote is genuine competition for the electoral vote as a means of achieving political power. Normative expectations may lead to incorrect identification of ills in the body politic. For instance, many voters are ignorant, irrational, and biased, yet nonetheless are not pathological constituents of the body politic. Many voters do not know what the issues are, but they can and do participate in conferring power. Election issues are not so much the major questions of public policy as they are instruments of competition, and since the election does not determine public policy but those who will make

---

[7] An excellent summary and evaluation of these normative theory specifications may be found in Bernard Berelson, "Democratic Theory and Public Opinion," *Public Opinion Quarterly*, 16 (Fall, 1952), 313–30.

public policy, the lack of issue orientation on the part of the population is not pathological.

Electoral competition has its own built-in control on techniques
used. Techniques that succeed will probably be used again, but the
fact that others compete against the user of such techniques serves
to set limits on their selection. Abstract morality or electoral in-
telligence are not in themselves restraints on the selection of techniques. Empirical calculations as to the anticipated success or failure
resulting from the use of selected techniques is a far more effective
control.

In summary, then, consider the following statement by Murray B.
Levin on the nature of the electorate and its role:

Most citizens do not and cannot play an active role or display the sustained
interest in politics required of them by the [classical democratic] theory.
The majority do not engage in true discussion, are not well informed or
motivated, and do not vote on the basis of principles. . . . The theory also
fails to account for the necessary roles of leadership and exaggerates the
active role of the masses. Those who do lead are therefore regarded as potential usurpers of what rightfully belongs to the electorate. The theory
also leads its followers to believe that the bargaining and compromising,
which is so essential to democratic politics, is necessarily evil. In short, the
roles as defined by eighteenth-century democratic theory are too demanding and the political structure designed to implement them cannot be what
it is supposed to be. . . . If individuals continue to believe in the classical
view, they will feel politically alienated.[8]

The Role of Political Parties

Political parties are organizations created to assist in first winning
and then maintaining power through the electoral process, to serve
as instruments of the competitive struggle for political power. As
Clinton Rossiter says,

The primary function of a political party in a democracy such as ours is to
control and direct the struggle for power. From this function all others de-
rive naturally. . . . It is one of the aspirations of democracy to bring this
struggle as much as possible into the open. It is the great purpose of
political parties, the handmaidens of democracy, to bring the struggle under
control; to institutionalize it with organization, to channel it through nomi-
nations and elections, to publicize it by means of platforms and appeals,
above all to stabilize it in the form of that traditional quadrille in which

---

[8] *The Alienated Voter: Politics in Boston* (New York: Holt, Rinehart & Winston, Inc., 1960), pp. 73–4.

the Ins and the Outs change places from time to time on a signal from the voters.[9]

Political parties have no functions independent of this primary role. They do many other things, such as enlighten and educate the voters, but these are subsidiary to their primary function. Thus many of the alleged failures of American political parties are not failures at all; setting arbitrary requirements as to what parties are supposed to do and then judging them deficient because they do not do these things is not realistic. What parties must do is rationalize the process of competition for the voters' approval; judgments as to their success must be made in terms of their effectiveness in winning elections.

American political parties tend to gravitate toward a moderate stand on issues and are not readily identified on an ideological conservative-liberal spectrum. The parties must maximize their appeal to the greatest possible number of voters; they are not established to distinguish between ideological positions, and knowledgeable politicians are aware of this. The 1964 presidential election is a case in point. The Republican Party was moved to differentiate itself from the Democratic Party in a futile effort to give the voter "a choice for a change." To the extent that the party did this—differentiated its positions from those that had been appealing successfully to the American electorate for three decades—it did not compete effectively for the votes of the electorate. The 1964 presidential election was, then, only formally competitive, in that the Democratic nominee was not forced by the other party to compete seriously by defending his position or challenging that of the Republican nominee.

While the political party serves as the chief instrument of organization and conduct of competition for power, many other things are accomplished. Parties select the candidates, sorting out from all potential ones those who will maximize the possibilities of winning. Furthermore, parties serve to single out individuals for participation, both in the campaign and in the government, either as members of the winning side (the Administration) or as members of the opposition within government. Parties also articulate positions on questions of public policy during and after election campaigns, as part of both government and opposition. They provide identification and continuity for the involvement of individuals and groups in the political process. They serve as instruments of the responsibility of public officials to the electorate. They serve as organizers and conductors

[9] *Parties and Politics in America* (Ithaca, N.Y.: Cornell University Press, 1960), p. 39.

of public policy and as institutionalized means of challenge to that policy. These other activities follow directly from their primary role of serving as a basic means of competition for political power.

Once the election is over, the party becomes a means of continuing the competition for political power. For those who won and are in policymaking positions, the party is an instrument of government; for those who lost, the party is an instrument of opposition. In both cases, however, the role of party does not essentially change, although its techniques do. The party must still maximize the possibility of its victory in future elections.

Parties do differ; the records of the parties as to electoral appeal, success, and policy commitment are not beyond specification.[10] Party adherence (the regularity of certain types of voters supporting a given party) is a major source of the data available in analyzing the results of, not reasons for, the existence of the parties, and it reflects differences in the techniques of the parties in carrying out their primary function.

Parties cannot represent policies and issues in specific detail. They tend to fuse issues and policy questions into easily manipulated generalizations rather than to break them down into specific, manageable parts. They tend to frame policy questions in terms of symbols such as peace, prosperity, honesty, efficiency, high standard of living, democracy, rather than in concrete questions of the interests involved and the effect of alternative policies on these interests.

The Role of Interest Groups

While parties are obliged to seek as broad a base of support from as many divergent groups as possible, interest groups are organized to represent a particular and limited clientele. Consequently, interest groups are not structured to maximize the possibility of winning in elections. They are nevertheless important as major potential support groups that must be competed for by the parties during campaigns and listened to by officeholders.

Political interest groups are important adjuncts to the formal process of representation. Since elections cannot give specific answers to the multitude of questions upon which decisions must be made by those in power, policymakers must communicate with the major interests in society having a stake in particular issues. Public policy

[10] See, for example, Rossiter, Chap. III, "Democrats and Republicans: Who Are They?" and Chap. IV, "Democrats and Republicans: What Difference Does It Make?," pp. 66–150.

is the outgrowth of the process of accommodating these various interests. Politics is the business of representing the conflicting, sometimes overlapping, often diametrically opposed interests of various groups. Interest groups feed information to the policymakers, who use it to make decisions and to calculate the impact of these decisions upon their chances of staying in office. We no longer need to posit, as did the classical theorists, the existence of a general will or public opinion representative of what the people want. What we now recognize as public interest grows out of the conflicting interests of various groups and is a product of the rationalization, compromise, and accommodation of these interests.

We have already considered in Chapter 1 how interest groups institutionalize advantages for themselves in constitutional documents. They are also quite successful in representing various viewpoints on and assessments of the desirability of alternative policies before legislative, executive, and judicial bodies at all levels.

Special interest groups at the local level are active in the areas of health regulations, education, crime and police, fire protection, planning and zoning, transportation, and similar services. At the state level public utilities, liquor and agricultural interests, and an ill-defined but nonetheless important "urban interest" are well represented by such groups. Among the most common are leagues of women voters, civic groups, taxpayers' associations, chambers of commerce, manufacturing and teachers' organizations, labor unions, railroad and trucking interests, oil producers, municipal leagues and organizations of county officials, newspapers, and religious groups, to name only some of the most significant.

The ease with which those who have special interests can gain access to policymakers at state and local levels is an important indicator of the representativeness of the policymakers. An average citizen, an individual who has something on his mind, can be heard—through letters to his councilman or legislator, visits to the offices of an administrative agency, letters to the editor, and the like—but the major influence on public policy comes from organized political interest groups. These used to be called pressure groups, a term that is misleading because it connotes a kind of political armtwisting. The representatives of such groups, often called lobbyists for their traditional operations in the lobby of legislatures, have a positive role in representation. They transmit to the policymakers the demands of their various publics, providing firsthand information on their constituents' view of specific matters. They provide detailed background material for proposed legislation. They also provide evaluations as to the effect of various proposals on the welfare of their interest group, the broader welfare of the locality or state, and the political welfare of the policymaker himself.

Political interest groups are very much concerned with the outcome of elections; if people who favor their interests are elected to the local council or to the state legislature, their chances of success in influencing public policy will be enhanced. However, the representatives of such groups normally do not concentrate on electing people to office or attempt to gain public office themselves; rather, they attempt to influence those who hold public office. In this role they represent the most highly articulated and organized extragovernmental agency for influencing public policy. Their access to the legislature, local council, or county governing body ensures that there will be a continuous adjustment of conflicting interests, an important addition to the formal process of representation through election.

Political interest groups also have access to administrative policymakers at state and local levels. Since administrators often formulate policy proposals later presented to the local council or state legislature for formalization into law, political interest groups seek access in this prelegislative stage. They also seek access in the postlegislative stage, when the state or local administrators are implementing the broad policy determined by the local council or state legislature. They also have frequent access to judicial policymakers, although through considerably different means, which will be examined in greater detail in Chapter 7. Failure to recognize the intimate relationship between political interest groups and public policymaking, and the importance of these interests in the politics of the state will result in a naive and misleading picture of the political process in our state and local subsystems.

4

State and Local Politics and Participation

Politics in state and local governments varies widely. Generalization is virtually impossible, except with the clear proviso that the variations may be so significant as to make the generalization all but meaningless. While it is thus both impossible and undesirable to attempt any description of political procedures and structures except in broadest terms, certain patterns in the political subsystems can be identified that bear directly upon the way in which state and local politics relates to the theoretical considerations emphasized in Chapter 3. The reader is invited to make specific applications to the politics of his own state and to refer to the extensive literature concerning the politics of most states.

Characteristics of State and Local Politics

Certain general characteristics can be found in the politics of the states and most local communities. We have already noted that politics is essentially local. Now it is important to note first that the state closely supervises and controls the political process. Elections and related activities are matters peculiarly within the province of the states and not the national government. While Congress exercises some controls over elections, the major questions about candidates, campaigns, registration, voting, and election procedures are left for the state government to determine. Elaborate statutes and constitutional provisions exist, providing the legal framework for determining party structure; dates of elections; procedures for registering voters and conducting elections; qualifications for party membership; voter qualifications; number, composition, functions, and powers of various party officials and committees; nominating procedures; how and when a party may rightly call itself one and how it shall conduct itself; the conditions under which funds may be spent in campaigns; and who may contribute and in what circumstances. Regulations vary by state, but this list is fairly typical. Political parties and electoral procedures are essentially state mechanisms, and such regulations insure that they operate within the rules laid down by the constitution and legislature. The game of politics is not a private one.

A second general characteristic is decentralization of politics. We have already noted that national politics is really a conglomeration of independent state and local political structures gathering together periodically and purposely to elect national candidates. It is likewise true that state parties are more or less structured cooperative efforts of a highly decentralized conglomerate of local parties. In most states party power resides in local politics. Furthermore, since political power is primarily related to the ability to gain office, or to assist in others gaining office, and since gaining office is related to a constituency located in a given territory, it is not surprising that political power in the state is most often directly related to a local constituency. It is a fact of political life that control of the grass roots organization is essential to success in politics.

A third characteristic of state and local politics is the existence and importance of extralegal political organizations. By themselves the orderly structures regulated by state laws may be misleading, for they often mask and are supplemented by a wide variety of pseudo official yet quite permanent political organizations attaching themselves to the political party or the politicians or both. Failure to examine and to recognize these structures leads to a highly unsophisticated view of the political process in the states.

The predominance of the two-party pattern is a fourth characteristic of state and local politics. However, it is more prevalent in belief than actual practice, for many states do not have meaningfully competitive two-party systems. On the other hand, although many states have only one official party on the ballot (or have only one with a chance to win), few if any states are genuinely noncompetitive in their political struggles. Most of the so-called one-party states have genuine intraparty conflict. While apparently the easiest way to insure genuine competition for political power is to have two comparatively equal parties vying for power, it is nonetheless true that in the long run competition seems to exist in all the states (although domination by a so-called political machine or dynasty has sometimes occurred). The intensity of intraparty warfare, however, seems to match the intensity of interparty warfare.

A corollary to this structure of competition, and a partial explanation for its existence even in "one-party" states, is the multigroup character of political parties. These parties are not philosophically or theoretically oriented; they are amalgamations of widely divergent groups joining together for the specific purpose of electing officials to office in order to maximize their interests. Party platforms are the umbrellas under which these amalgamations take place, and appeals to narrow philosophical or economic interests are rarely resorted to and even more rarely successful in electing candidates. The multigroup character of the parties ensures, or at least promotes, competitiveness within the party.

A fifth characteristic of state and local politics is the frequent division of party control between the legislative and executive branches. Often the legislative branch is controlled by one party and the executive by another. Consequently, in most states it is not possible to talk about an administration in the sense that an administration is responsible for the overall business of governing the state. The governor is, nonetheless, thought of as the titular head of the government, and may be held responsible in political campaigns for what happens in the state. But in reality the division of power in the state is usually such that there is no way to hold one party responsible for the government.

Another characteristic, one we shall look at again in Chapter 5, is the almost universal lack of both sharp intraparty cohesion and interparty division in state legislatures. Most seem to divide more according to urban-rural, agricultural-industrial, north-south, or other economic or social characteristics than according to party affiliation.

Possibly the only valid generalization to be offered about state and local politics is that each state develops its own particular pattern of relationships. The serious reader will, when analyzing the political arrangements of his own state, test them to determine the extent to which they promote open competition for political power in which all those in the political arena have a real opportunity to participate; that is, he will test them to see how they conform to a meaningful democratic theory.

Two special concerns now require our attention. The myth of grass roots democracy and the affection for municipal reform are among the most persistent ingredients of local politics. A consideration of them would be justified by that fact alone, but their intimate relationship to the theoretical considerations discussed in Chapter 3 makes their examination even more to the point.

Grass Roots Democracy

The myth of the superiority of small town democracy is one of the most persistent in American tradition. Whether used to defend the

small town, to condemn the tendency toward centralization, or to
promote the virtues of state and local government generally, this
notion holds that (1) democracy works best at the lowest governmental level, (2) the prerequisites of democratic government exist
most clearly at the local level, and (3) the benefits of democratic involvement are realized in inverse relationship to size. It is a cliché
of political discourse that the growth of government diminishes the
chances of democracy. And it follows in this analysis that the instruments of politics—parties, political interest groups, elections, electorates—are healthiest at the local level and yet, paradoxically, less
necessary because of the superiority of democratic procedures at that
level.

Faith in grass roots democracy has little to support it. There is no
evidence that democracy works better in small communities or that
the characteristics of government and community at the local level
are such that democratic procedures are encouraged. Indeed, evidence
points in the opposite direction. Open competition for political power
is difficult if not impossible in many local communities.

While great size is no guarantee of democratic political processes,
conditions promoting competition are not maximized in the largely
homogeneous climate of the small town. The alleged virtues of small
towns—community of interest, lack of divisive elements, intimacy of
face-to-face relations, interdependence, common goals and values,
shared beliefs and customs, in short, as Robert C. Wood [1] terms it,
"fraternity"—are precisely the characteristics that make the democratic process highly unlikely if not impossible. Small towns are not
usually noted for their ability to generate, and most certainly not
noted for their willingness to tolerate, the kind of social-political
climate in which genuinely open competition for power can flourish.
Furthermore, corruption, crime, malfeasance in office, graft, and a
multitude of political if not moral sins have been far more prevalent
at the city and county level than at the state or national level. In fact,
it appears that problems of this character increase as the size of the
political community decreases. Democracy and localism in politics are
not coterminous. Although it is useful to politicians, the myth identifying democracy with localism contributes little to an understanding
of the way democracy operates in our states and localities.[2]

In view of the population trends of the last half century, examined in

---

[1] *Suburbia: Its People and Their Politics* (Boston: Houghton Mifflin Company, 1958), pp. 259–91.

[2] See also Roscoe C. Martin, *Grass Roots* (University, Ala.: University of
Alabama Press, 1957).

Chapter 2, it is fortunate that grass roots democracy is not an accurate portrayal of the requirements of democracy. If it were, the future of democracy in the United States would be dim, for we have not fit the small town model for the better part of the last century. On the other hand, in what seems to be a paradox, the instruments of that democratic process are largely local in nature. Furthermore, since most of the people live in urban areas, the political struggles affecting local government are apt to be most important to the day-to-day life of the citizen. Obviously, to understand the way the political system operates, one must understand the way those political institutions operate at the local and state levels; but to assume that only these subsystems are capable of attaining democratic character is both incorrect and misleading.

Local Political Reform

In Chapter 2 we discussed the efforts of contemporary reformers in the metropolitan area, which are largely devoted to suggesting and constructing consolidated metropolitan government. It was noted that there are significant differences between these metropolitan reformers and the older municipal reformers. At this point it is pertinent to discuss that older political reform movement primarily because of its political consequences. Its impact upon state and local politics has been a lasting one, reflected in both attitudes toward politics and institutional arrangements.

Municipal reform has been principally directed toward ridding the city of the evils of political corruption, a dominant theme in most states since the turn of the century.[3] The reformers had a commendable concern for making government and democracy workable at the local level. Unfortunately, many of them understood little about democracy and even less about politics and its role in a democratic system. Their basic assumptions—that politics and politicians are at best necessary evils not genuinely identified with the public welfare, and that good government could best be attained through application of business principles—are manifested in the major reforms advocated, and in some instances adopted. These include elimination of political parties, election by nonpartisan ballot, substitution of the collegial commission form of government for the more avowedly political mayor-council form, substitution of a professional administrator

---

[3] See Scott Greer, *Metropolitics* (New York: John Wiley & Sons, Inc., 1963); also Edward C. Banfield and James Q. Wilson, *City Politics* (Cambridge, Mass.: Harvard University Press, 1963), Chap. 11, "Reform," pp. 138–50.

(city manager) for a politically elected mayor, proportional representation, the initiative, referendum, and recall (to give the citizen direct participation and a means to control the politicians), improved procedures for budgeting, accounting, and fiscal controls, and various other institutional and procedural arrangements.

Since its heyday in the first twenty years of this century, the reform movement has declined, but many of the proposals mentioned above have remained as valuable contributions to government at the local level, for example, the improved budgeting, accounting, and other fiscal procedures, and the increased concern for professionalism and administrative competence.

The most characteristic effort of the reformers was to advocate local nonpartisanship and nonpolitical city government forms. Today, approximately 60 percent of all cities have nonpartisan elections, which means candidates for public office are not openly identified with a political party.[4] This practice is so firmly entrenched that it virtually would be political suicide in many communities for a politician to suggest its abolition, and academicians who question its value invite indignant condemnation from citizen and politician alike. Even seasoned politicians find it expedient to recommend local nonpartisanship. Coupled closely with the aim of ridding the city of the evil of politics through nonpartisan elections has been the adoption of nonpolitical forms of city government. Since the mayor-council arrangement was closely identified with strong political bosses in American cities, the commission system, in which there is a collegial body and no single executive, and the city-manager form, in which the executive is an administrative expert hired by the city council, promised to fulfill the demands for government free of politics.

To the extent that these innovations have increased expertise and administrative competence *without* eliminating politics, they have been valuable improvements. But they have succeeded in giving some communities local government without the dynamics of political control, or more frequently, politics has been hidden beneath the aura of respectability called nonpartisanship and expertise. These reforms also have reinforced the attitude that politics and political involvement are undesirable. They have contributed to a kind of schizophrenia in the body politic in which the prime necessity of a democratic system—open, deliberate competition for power—is viewed by many as a perversion of that system.

---

[4] See Charles R. Adrian, "Some General Characteristics of Nonpartisan Elections," *American Political Science Review*, 46 (September, 1952), 766–76, who suggests eleven propositions characteristic of nonpartisanship.

Few big cities have nonpartisan elections or nonpolitical forms of government, and only Nebraska and Minnesota elect their legislatures on a nonpartisan basis. The main reason has been that such solutions are inappropriate for such governments. Although nonpartisanship and its institutional corollaries work in many cities, the premises upon which these reforms are based, the analysis of the requirements of the political democracy from which they follow, lead to the untenable proposition that democracy can work best when politics and the political struggle are defined as alien to good government. Yet the open competition for political power is precisely what is at the center of the democratic process. Although by no means a guarantee, it is this that makes government and public policy reflect the demands of the people.

In recent years we have learned much about politics. We have learned that to understand politics in America we must understand it at the state and local levels, and to understand the politics of a state we must be able to identify the power structure in the local community.[5] There are many in the community who wield power, influence public policy, affect the business of governing, but who do not hold public office and are not politicians in the traditional sense. Correctly viewed, the political arena includes not only the politicians in office, those who run and their confidants, but also businessmen, academicians, civic leaders, newspaper editors, ministers, labor leaders, and, to their chagrin, the municipal reformers themselves. The effort to eliminate politics, to control politicians through depoliticizing elections, and to structure government so as to elevate the expert, misses the crucial point that politics at the local level is inherent to the democratic process itself. There can be, in short, no really nonpartisan or nonpolitical democratic government at any level.

Political Party Organization

To outline the organization and structure of political parties is to suggest a uniformity that is nonexistent. Nevertheless, it is possible

[5] See Robert A. Dahl, *Who Governs?* (New Haven, Conn.: Yale University Press, 1961); Floyd Hunter, *Community Power Structure* (Chapel Hill, N.C.: University of North Carolina Press, 1953); Herbert Kaufman and Victor Jones, "The Mystery of Power," *Public Administration Review,* XIV (Summer, 1954), 205–12; Peter H. Rossi, "Power and Community Structure," *Midwest Journal of Political Science,* IV (November, 1960), 390–401; Edward C. Banfield, *Political Influence* (New York: The Free Press, 1961); and M. Kent Jennings, *Community Influentials* (New York: The Free Press, 1964).

to indicate a pattern, recognizing that there will be deviations from it in everything but the essentials.

A typical state party organization, to begin at the bottom, involves organization at the precinct level. Precincts are voting districts, usually quite small and limited to a neighborhood or small section of a town. There is usually a precinct committeeman or captain whose major job is to keep contact with the voters, to get them registered, to discover "popular demands," and to deliver the vote on election day. He also serves on the next higher level county committee. In many states there is a wide variety of local committees. The functions assigned to these are legion, and the means of selecting them—primaries, conventions, or caucuses—also numerous. Their primary functions, however, are the same: to keep contact directly with the voter, to do the "nitty-gritty" business of advancing the interests of the party and its candidates, and to deliver the vote.

In most states the next level in party organization is the county central committee. In some states, particularly those with large urban areas, there may be an intermediate level between the precinct and the county, such as ward committee, city committee, state legislative district committee, or congressional district committee. Each may have membership on the county committee. In most states the county committee directs the party's activities. It raises money, secures candidates, organizes and conducts campaigns, recruits members, handles patronage dispensation, and does all the things necessary to consolidate political power.

At the apex of the state party structure is the state central committee, usually chosen through party primaries or by state party convention, although occasionally it is selected by the county or some intermediate committees. There is no uniformity in the size of the state central committee, ranging from about a dozen to several hundred. In general it oversees all activities of the party, assists the county committees in directing local campaigns, raises money for and assists in the election of candidates for state office, coordinates patronage, and generally involves itself in the functioning of the party on a state-wide basis. It coordinates and assists rather than directs and controls because of the high degree of decentralization of most state party organizations. V. O. Key, one of the best known commentators on party structure at the state level, summarized it this way:

The party organization is sometimes regarded as a hierarchy based on the precinct executive capped by the national committee, but it may be more accurately described as a system of layers of organization. Each successive layer—county or city, state, national—has an independent concern about elections in its geographical jurisdiction. Yet each higher level of organization, to accomplish its ends, must obtain the collaboration of the lower layer or layers of organization. That collaboration comes about, to the extent that it does come about, through a sense of common cause rather than by the exercise of command.[6]

Although not an official part of the structure of a political party, the candidates and their entourages are in most states the most important part of the political organization. They carry the major load of directing campaigns, raising money, recruiting voters, and taking care of all the other activities necessary to compete effectively against rival candidates. Frequently assisting (and some would say sometimes interfering with) the candidates and the formal party structure is a large number of extralegal informal organizations, sometimes called political clubs, often representing various splinter groups or competing political philosophies within the same party. It is in these informal structures that many people find their most congenial political home.

Superimposed upon the formal and informal party structure may be "machines," which command the loyalty of party regulars to such an extent that they control most of the local and county committees. Notable among such groups was that of Huey Long in Louisiana in the 1920s and 1930s and that of Harry Byrd in Virginia until the 1960s. Some would include the Dewey organization in New York in the 1940s and the Humphrey organization in Minnesota in the 1950s and 1960s. The best known machines, however, have been at the local level—Tammany Hall in New York City,[7] Green in Philadelphia, Daley in Chicago, Crump in Memphis, and Abe Ruef in San Francisco, for example. The existence of extraparty political machines seems to be possible not only in one-party states but in highly competitive two-party states as well.

Registration and Voting Procedures

Practically all states determine who is eligible to vote through some sort of registration requirement. This is to insure that prior to the election those who wish to vote have been checked as to their qualifications and have had their names included on a list of qualified voters. Registration may be either permanent or periodic, and it

[6] *Politics, Parties, and Pressure Groups*, 5th ed. (New York: Thomas Y. Crowell Company, 1964), p. 316.

[7] Edward J. Flynn, *You're The Boss* (New York: Collier Books, 1962). Flynn was "boss" of the Bronx for 25 years.

usually requires the voter to appear in person to register. In some states failure to vote in a given election will void the registration, thus necessitating re-registration if the voter is to participate in the next election. While the registration system is generally regarded as necessary to minimize the possibility of fraud or illegal voting, it has been criticized as unduly inconvenient to the voter, thus discouraging him from participating. In fact, large numbers of people do fail to register and thus are not eligible to vote on election day.

The most important considerations are the requirements that must be met before one can vote. They generally include the following: prior registration; attainment of a minimum age, usually twenty-one; [8] United States citizenship; a prescribed length of residence in the state and usually in the precinct; absence of conviction for serious crimes; sanity; and in a few states an education or literacy test. Two requirements, now in disuse, were the property test and the poll tax, but many states still require one to be a property holder to vote on public bond issues. The Twenty-Fourth Amendment to the United States Constitution, ratified in 1964, outlawed the poll tax as a requirement for voting in national elections.

Most of these requirements can be defended as legitimate means to insure that the electoral process includes only voters who are at least minimally qualified to exercise the franchise. However, there is no universally agreed upon meaning for the phrase "minimally qualified to vote." It is equally true that some of these requirements have been imposed to restrict participation of "unacceptables," to insure that they have no chance to win. Indeed, it is extremely hard to establish that age twenty-one or nineteen or eighteen is an appropriate measure of qualification to vote. Likewise, it is not empirically verifiable that one must know how to read and write in order to participate in the selection of governors. The important thing to notice, as we emphasized in Chapter 3, is that for the political process to be genuinely competitive, unrestricted participation, that is, the ability to compete must be protected by the guarantee that all who wish to may do so with a meaningful chance of being able to win. This presumes that no potential competitors will be told they are not allowed to compete. Insofar as they are prohibited from competing, the question the election was to answer has been begged—the competitive struggle has been foreclosed to some, and the outcome has been partially predetermined. To this extent it is a noncompetitive or at least a restricted competitive system, differing only in degree from the closed systems in which some elite group—the party, the church,

[8] But in Georgia and Kentucky 18, Alaska 19, and Hawaii 20.

the privileged class, the favored race—reserves to itself the guarantee
of success.

No such rigid exclusions are operative in the states today, but in
the past participation has been restricted. Elaborate procedures to
preclude Negro voting in many states are familiar evidence of such
restriction on participation. Denial of access to political power
through legitimate channels may encourage, even invite, extralegal
efforts. Consequently, such restrictions must be carefully evaluated
and not merely assumed to be satisfactory because of historical prece-
dent or momentary emotion.

Selecting and Electing Candidates

Although the democratic process requires that all potential competitors for political power be allowed to compete, it is obvious that
not everyone may run for office and appear on the ballot. Political
parties must keep the number of potential candidates down so that
they can compete effectively. In most states two candidates run, one
for each of the competing parties. Sometimes there are more candidates, one from each of several parties able to get on the ballot, or,
in the case of the one-party states, several from various competing
factions of the party. Most of the elimination is made as the result
of intangibles such as influence and power, the existence of which is
easily attested to but not easily demonstrated empirically. But the
legal procedures in the states promote the polarization of choice by
imposing procedures and qualifications that must be met before one
may be an official candidate for office.

Most important of these procedures is the direct primary. All states
use the direct primary for nominating candidates for at least some
state offices, although some states allow conventions to select nominees. In addition, many states permit alternative means to designate
candidates for local offices. The direct primary is a kind of pre-election,
in which those who wish to be party nominees (and who have met
other statutory requirements, such as a fairly generally required
petition with the prescribed number of voters' signatures attached)
submit themselves to the electorate of the party for determining
which one shall represent the party in the general election. Usually
this is a *closed* primary, in which the voters are only those who have in
the registration process indicated their affiliation with the party holding the primary. In seven states the primary is *open*, meaning a voter
may take part in the primary of whichever party he chooses without
indicating party preference. One state (Washington) uses the "blan-

ket primary," with the voter being allowed to indicate his preferences in both parties. The usual pattern, however, is to allow a voter to participate only in the primary of his own party. Primaries are provided for and controlled by state law and are an integral part of the electoral process. Obviously, in a one-party state victory in the primary is tantamount to election to office.

All states have a secret ballot. Procedures for casting the ballot vary widely, but the usual methods are by written ballot or voting machine. The costs of conducting a campaign for a primary or a general election have become staggering. It is not unusual for an election in a large city to cost between $.5 million and $1.5 million and for a gubernatorial election in a larger state to cost well over $2 million. The intensified use of television, jet air travel, public relations firms, and extensive, private poll-taking organizations promise to make these figures increase substantially. Indeed, the cost of elections, and the potential political importance of those who can provide the funds for campaigns, constitute very serious concerns today.

Voter Participation

The amount of voter participation in our states is a most important consideration in seeking to understand our political system. The factors we have already spoken of—registration, voting requirements, party structure—may contribute significantly to the degree of participation, but we will know very little about state and local politics unless we know a great deal about who participates, and under what circumstances. The literature is growing, and an encouraging amount of empirical data is now available. Lester Milbrath has made this statement:

About one-third of the American adult population can be characterized as politically apathetic or passive; in most cases they are unaware, literally, of the political part of the world around them. Another 60 percent play largely spectator roles in the political process; they watch, they cheer, they vote, but they do not do battle. Only about 5 to 7 percent can be characterized as political gladiators. These proportions apply mainly to elections at which a President is chosen in the United States. The apathetic ranks probably are even larger in strictly state and local elections.[9]

In the literature there is much discussion about this noninvolvement in politics, the general conclusion being that somehow it is

[9] "Political Participation in the States," in Herbert Jacob and Kenneth N. Vines (eds.), *Politics in the American States* (Boston: Little, Brown & Company, 1965), p. 29.

pathological in a democracy. However, much of the disillusionment stems from the inability of the process in action to meet the expectations generated by the process in theory. Political alienation (an extreme form of nonparticipation), nonparticipation, and scepticism reflect not so much pathology in practice as pathology in the theory of democracy. As E. E. Schattschneider says,

> We become cynical about democracy because the public does not act the way the simplistic definition of democracy says it should act, or we try to whip the public into doing things it does not want to do, is unable to do and has too much sense to do. The crisis here is not a crisis in democracy but a crisis in theory.[10]

Or, as Murray Levin notes,

> Feelings of political alienation will arise when the political role that an individual expects to play and believes is rightfully his cannot be realized. . . .
> Feelings of alienation will arise in individuals who accept the classical democratic theory because it demands more of the individual citizen than he can realistically fulfill and promises more than can be delivered.[11]

Although nonparticipation, withdrawal, or alienation from the political process are serious problems, they are not necessarily pathological ingredients in a democracy. It is a fact of political life that many people simply will not become actively involved in politics; it is also a fact that a democracy does not require everyone to participate. Just how many people must participate we do not know, but what we must have is competition to get people to participate in the selection of those who seek political power. An understanding of this reality—that nonparticipation is not necessarily pathological— helps to avoid the frustration and alienation so often resulting from an awareness that many of the expectations of traditional democratic theory are not verifiable in experience. Many of the "perversions" of democracy are in fact normal parts of an operable democratic process, often identified as pathological simply because they do not conform to the prescriptions of a democratic theory that itself does not conform to reality. If the political process in our states does not operate as reflected in traditional theory, for example, if a large part of the population does not participate and does not seem interested in par-

---

[10] E. E. Schattschneider, *The Semisovereign People* (New York: Holt, Rinehart & Winston, Inc., 1960), p. 134.

[11] Murray B. Levin, *The Alienated Voter* (New York: Holt, Rinehart & Winston, Inc., 1960), pp. 72–3.

ticipating, it is not because there is something wrong with our democracy but because our theoretical model is inaccurate or misleading.

In sum, then, while we may wish to involve greater numbers of people in politics, it is not necessarily dangerous or undesirable that they are not. What is important is that those who will participate be actively competed for, so that no one is allowed to govern without having won the privilege in a competition for the electorate's approval. It is particularly important to insure that the nonactive or nonparticipating are available to respond to the efforts of those who are competing for their support. If, however, they are precluded from the possibility of operating within the political process, as distinguished from being simply uninterested in participating, this would be a serious restriction on competition. There is a significant difference between concern because people do not want to participate and consequently do not vote and concern because people cannot participate even if they want to respond to campaigners' appeals.

There is another aspect of this problem that is sometimes overlooked—the kinds of political participation available. Most of our data, and thus much of our discussion concerning participation has to do with such direct participation as voting. It is a fact that a large number of people do not vote. But there are many other kinds of political participation, some quite important in the competition for political power. Among them are the following: being aware of political stimuli, even in the absence of a physical act such as voting; exchanging views, discussing, involving oneself through communication; contributing money or time; influencing close friends and acquaintances; attending political meetings; participating in demonstrations and public protests; writing letters to officeholders; and, indeed, in some circumstances refusing to vote or participate (a kind of negative participation that is as indicative of attitude and as important to the outcome of competition for power as most forms of positive activity). What we must know is not that people do not participate but why, for the answer to this question will allow those competing for political office to extend their appeals to the nonparticipants, thus enlarging the competition.

The efforts of campaigners to appeal to certain people and thus to get their support cannot be entirely successful, however, if arbitrary restraints are placed upon the participation of those people. Some of our election procedures operate both to make it impossible for large segments of the population to participate and to discourage others, regardless of how attractive the competitors' appeals may be. For instance, for most of the last one hundred years the efforts of the American Negro to vote and otherwise to participate politically have been seriously curtailed by both legal and extralegal mechanisms. Such arbitrary restraint is a serious restriction on the competitiveness of the political process. Likewise, many states make it difficult for third or splinter parties to get on the ballot by imposing strict requirements such as a very high number of signatures on a petition, another restriction on the ability to participate. The excessive number of elections in which voters are expected to participate may also deter many from active participation, as does the overly long ballot in most state and local elections. Both impose unrealistic demands on the voter and may cause him to reject the process entirely. The reasons why persons cannot vote, in terms of the unattractiveness or inappropriateness of the competitors' appeals and techniques, or of arbitrary restraints on participation, need to be evaluated once one understands the relationship of participation to the democratic process.

There are many arenas for participation in the politics of state and local government. This chapter has concentrated on participation in the selection of those who govern; the next three chapters focus on participation in the policymaking processes in three different arenas— the legislative, the executive, and the judicial.

5

Policymaking Arenas: Legislative Bodies

The concern of the next three chapters is how public policy is made in the various states and local communities. This involves an attempt to identify common ingredients and similarities in the policymaking process, to discover the overall pattern through which policy is developed. To do this we must first examine the nature of the policymaking process and the problem of representation.

Nature of the Policymaking Process

Public policymaking cannot be considered synonymous with lawmaking. Lawmaking, defined as the passing of statutes by a legislative body, is simply one manifestation of public policy. Some expressions of public policy have the force of law while others are simply expressions of publicly declared purposes or aims. They include official policy statements, executive orders, administrative rules, adjudications made by administrative hearing boards, and decisions of courts.

Public policy can emanate from the executive and judicial branches as well as the legislative branch. However, some agencies, such as legislatures—congress, state legislatures, city councils, county boards of supervisors or commissioners—are engaged extensively and continuously in the process of developing policy relative to a wide range of problems. Others, such as administrative agencies, make policy pronouncements in comparatively limited spheres but with broad implications and effects. Still others, such as the courts, make infrequent policy pronouncements almost always incidental to carrying out nonpolicymaking activities. All, however, are on occasion pronouncing, modifying, or implementing policy.

Public policy is the determination of what government should or should not do about certain public problems. To put it another way, public policy in a democratic society is the nearest possible approximation of what the people want as expressed through imperfect mechanisms for representing their demands. Governmental institutions at all levels are engaged in translating public demands into policy. The effort may be imperfect, and the policy pronounced may not accurately reflect the demands of all the people, either because the demands defy rationalization in an articulate policy, or because the procedures for determining and translating them into policy are defective. In Chapter 3 we examined the roles of political parties, interest groups, and elections in determining demands; now we will examine the role of formal institutions of representation in the policymaking process.

Separation of Powers and Policymaking

A familiar aspect of our government is the separation of powers. As popularly understood, a deliberate and rational separation of powers exists among the three branches of government. The legislature makes the law, the executive agencies administer it, and the courts enforce and interpret it. There are checks and balances to insure the effectiveness of this separation and the continuing coequal status of the three branches. Through these checks and balances no one branch is able to monopolize power, yet each has the power to check the others when the danger of misusing power is present.

This picture is accurate but not complete. It tends to obscure the fact that there is more a separation of structures than of powers. Although comparatively highly structured at the national level, the separation of powers is often entirely absent at the local level. For instance, county government almost always lacks this separation between the executive and the legislative branches since the usual pattern is for the executive function to be performed by the legislative board of commissioners. Furthermore, two of the three major forms of city government reject this concept. The commission system concentrates executive and legislative power in the hands of the commission, which functions as the collegial executive, and the council-manager plan places both legislative and executive responsibility in the council, which hires a manager to administer the executive function. The judiciary, however, remains at all levels comparatively separate from the others. But the separate structures actually perform cooperative, interacting, and complementary activities. While none may monopolize the policymaking activity, none may uncompromisingly block the others. The critical point to remember is that this system of separate structures with interacting powers is really a system of "antagonistic cooperation."

Nature of Representation

Perhaps the central consideration in policymaking is representation, yet there has never been universal agreement as to the nature of representation. Is a governmental institution representative of the people only when it is selected by popular election? Can a court, for instance, be representative even though it is not elected and not subject to removal except by extraordinary procedures? For our discussion the three central ingredients of any system of representation are the methods by which the representatives are selected, their availability to those interested in affecting public policy, and the procedures and instruments for holding them accountable.

Selection

The legislative, executive, and judicial bodies in our states and local communities differ markedly as formal channels of representation, particularly in selection methods. All legislative bodies are elected; governors and mayors are elected, but the real executive in a council-manager system, the city manager, is appointed; most administrative agencies are appointive but in some states the heads of major administrative agencies are elected; and some courts are appointed, while large numbers are elected. It would be misleading to conclude that only those officials who are popularly elected are representative. Those who are appointed share in the close contact with the electorate, for the elected official responsible for appointing them knows that his appointees may seriously affect his and his associates chances of retaining office. On the other hand, the method of selection may provide comparative insulation, as in the case of the courts, from the immediate political repercussions of day-to-day activities. Evaluation depends upon the comparative weight to be given the two ingredients—political repercussion and political insulation.

Access

In Chapter 3 we suggested that the ease with which those who have special interests can gain access to the policymakers is an important indicator of their representativeness. The major influencers of public policy are the organized political interest groups, of which thousands are active at all levels of state and local government. These groups make their interests known to those who make public policy. They are an indispensable adjunct to the formal process of representation, which is elections.

Activities to influence the product of legislative bodies, whether a city council, a county board of supervisors or commissioners, or a state legislature, are generally familiar. Less familiar is the activity of interest groups with respect to executive or administrative policy-makers and the courts. Since administrators often formulate policy proposals that are later presented to the legislature for formalization into law, interest groups seek access at this prelegislative stage. They also seek access in the postlegislative stage when the administrators implement policy determinations made by the city council, county board, or state legislature. Interest groups tend to influence executive decisions in a variety of ways. Most are vitally concerned with appointments, for if they can influence the composition of public agencies the policy determinations of such agencies may be more easily influenced. Furthermore, access to these agencies may greatly affect the kinds of determinations the agencies make.

Access to judicial policymakers is further evidence of the complexity or pluralism of the representative system. Interest groups often find it desirable, sometimes because of their inability to compete effectively in the legislative, executive, and electoral arenas, to shift their efforts to the courts in attempting to modify public policy. Access here can be obtained in several ways: by affecting the choice of who will sit on the bench through the appointive process, or in those cases in which judges are elected, through helping to elect or defeat specific candidates, or through the professionals—lawyers— who serve as a special kind of "lobby" before the courts. Another highly effective means of access to the courts is the test case, through which those interested in challenging an established policy seek to have the courts invalidate or modify it. The *amicus curiae* ("friend of the court") brief submitted by parties outside the case in support of a party involved serves well to represent specific interests and positions before the courts.

Responsibility

Another aspect of representation that bears on policymaking at the state and local levels is responsibility. What procedures do we have at these levels to guarantee or to promote restraint and control on the policymakers?

Here again we must refer to the key role played by competition in the political system. While there is no evidence that an election is an appropriate instrument for making rational evaluations of the effectiveness of policymakers, the necessity of their competing for public office provides the means through which policymakers may be held politically responsible. In surveying the three government branches we should seek to understand how their methods of selection and operation relate them to the competitive electoral process so as to provide a measure of responsibility.

Elected officials—mayors, governors, members of city councils and state legislatures, county commissioners, and even in some cases judges or courts—are directly responsible through the electoral process. Any act by such an elected official may affect both his chances of reelection and the political future of his associates. He must, to some extent at least, make policy with an eye to election returns, past and prospective. He may and often does influence (some would say educate) the voters to respond favorably to his point of view, but he is forced to recognize that his competitors can also influence them. As long as he depends on votes for his right to office he must act responsibly—that is, within the limits of his constituents' tolerance.

Many state and local officials, on the other hand, are not elected. They do not depend directly upon the voters for office and the consequent authority to make policy decisions. But they are not thus exempt from responsibility. Here we must recognize that there is an indirect responsibility imposed upon appointive officials through the elected officials. Unfortunately a governor or mayor cannot always be held politically responsible for all that his administrators do or omit doing, and many administrative officials are virtually independent of direct control by the governor or mayor. However, elected officials must compete for public office partially on the record of the administrators, even though they are not legally responsible for these administrators. A state legislator or a city council member may often increase his chances for reelection through his success in controlling or criticizing administrators by vigorous challenge, investigation, personal contact, and other mechanisms available for reviewing administrative action.

Although there is no easy explanation of the way governmental institutions operate to insure representation in the formation of public policy, our understanding of policymaking will be increased if we understand the differences existing among the three governmental branches—differences in selection, access, and responsibility. The following discussions will provide material to make such comparisons and to assess the effectiveness of policymaking within these arenas.

State and Local Legislatures: Roles

We can understand legislative policymaking processes by first examining the roles of legislative bodies in general and then examining specifically the operation of the legislatures at the state level, and in county, city, and special district. Each of these governments has some type of legislative body and each has a set of roles distinguishable from those of other governing bodies at that level.

The most universally recognized, and obviously the most important, role of legislatures is to pass statutes, that is, *lawmaking*. The clearest manifestations of a legislative body in operation in any unit are its ordinances or statutes, which determine or control the conduct of members of that society. Additionally, in the process of considering and adopting legislation, it performs a very important role in *informing* the electorate. The legislative body focuses attention on major questions of public policy, debates, discusses, and serves as the catalyst for public opinion on important current issues. Much of what goes on in a legislature does not produce law, but the process contributes significantly to developing awareness in the general public and, more importantly, in officials holding office of what is and what might become policy.

This role as an open forum, as a sounding board, is complementary to another performed by the legislature, the *reconciliation of competing interests*. Public policy may be considered the result of such reconciliation, and the most formalized or institutionalized set of procedures for it is in the legislative body. Here, in any government, the various interests "lock horns," and as a result of the conflict and ensuing reconciliation of opposing positions policy is made. Much of this drama is not apparent to the casual observer, but to fail to recognize the conflict, dealing, and compromising that are part of the legislative operation, or to consider these pathological, is to fail to understand the legislative process.

We have already suggested that in many cases the statutes passed by legislative bodies are not necessarily original expressions of public policy. Often the legislature does not so much establish new policy as formalize and regularize policy developed somewhere in the administrative process of the government. Usually when a legislature considers a bill there has already been a considerable amount of political involvement by interests anxious to see the policy adopted. Much of this activity may have been directed toward influencing administrators. In many instances policy has already been established by nonlegislative agencies, which though they do not make law, do make, act upon, and cause others to act upon policy decisions. Thus a very real and important role of a legislature is to *legitimize decisions.*

Our brief consideration of the separation of powers suggests that *legislative oversight* of executive and administrative agencies, and to some extent judicial bodies, is a widely recognized role. The most useful mechanism of this role is to control appropriations, and much time is spent to determine the amount of money to be allocated for various public activities. But investigation, public hearing, and publicity are also very useful mechanisms by which the legislature exercises general supervision over executive agents. Another very important aspect of legislative control is the power of legislatures to approve appointments made by the executive. The upper house of most state legislatures is responsible for approving appointments made by the governor to various executive positions and to the courts, and many city councils have a similar responsibility for appointments made by the mayor.

There are other activities undertaken by legislative bodies, but the variety is so great as to defy precise categorization. For instance, most legislatures have a *constituent function;* they are responsible for making proposals for change in the constitutional document, either the state constitution or the city charter. Also, most legislative bodies engage in many *ceremonial activities*—recognizing visiting dignitaries, proclaiming special days of celebration, and similar ritualistic activity.

Organization, Structure, and Procedures

So far their discussion has centered on general roles of a legislature. These are equally applicable to the Congress, the state legislature, or the city council. However, there may be significant differences in the emphasis or comparative importance of one function or set of functions in the various governments. Obviously no two legislatures are exactly the same, and no local legislative bodies in one area are fully comparable to those in other parts of the country.

The four legislative bodies we are concerned with here are the state legislature, the county board of supervisors or commissioners, the city council, and the governing board of special districts. Our discussion of them will be directed toward understanding how each contributes to public policymaking.

Bicameral or Unicameral

The most universally recognized characteristic of state legislatures is their bicameral character; they are composed of two houses. The

Congress of the United States, with the Senate having equal representation from every state and the House of Representatives using
population as the basis of representation, was the model followed for
the creation of most state legislatures. In 1934, Nebraska changed
to a unicameral legislature, but no other state has abolished its
bicameral legislature. With the Supreme Court ruling in 1964 that the
Fourteenth Amendment requires both houses of a state legislature to
be apportioned according to population,[1] major changes have had to
be made in the composition of the houses in many states, but no state
has as yet even hinted at moving toward a unicameral legislature.

The case for bicameralism in state legislatures rests most heavily
on tradition. A bicameral arrangement is familiar and hence most
acceptable, and the federal experience with this type legislature,
originally adopted as a pragmatic compromise of a difficult problem
of representation faced by the framers of the Constitution, served as
a strong impetus for both the adoption of a bicameral system initially
and its defense historically.

Over the years, however, support for bicameralism has included
more than simple familiarity or traditional value. The most common
arguments for it include: (1) a bicameral structure allows for representation of different interests, both population and important geographic ones; (2) it guarantees a wiser legislative product by promoting more adequate consideration of issues and policies; (3) the delays
built into a bicameral system, in which both houses must approve in
identical form a piece of legislation before it becomes law, discourage
hasty and ill-considered legislation; (4) there is less opportunity or
likelihood for special interests to monopolize the legislative body; and
(5) there is a broader base of representation than is possible in a
unicameral legislature.

The opposition to bicameralism has never been widespread, although the older reform movement in the early part of the twentieth
century included in its catalog a unicameral state legislature. While
these reformers were notably ineffective in promoting such a change,
their arguments have become the standard opposition to bicameralism, namely: (1) two houses are unnecessary because they diffuse
responsibility, with one house being able to blame the other both for
failure to enact legislation and for the type of legislation enacted;
(2) legislative delay and obstruction is promoted; (3) "politics" is
increased through the additional opportunity to manipulate representational districts for political gain; and (4) the positive benefits of
the unicameral legislature are in themselves justification for a change.

[1] *Reynolds* v. *Sims,* 377 U.S. 533.

Among these alleged benefits are increased efficiency, more easily placed responsibility, attraction of more competent and professionally oriented public servants, protection against excessive political manipulation, and the saving of significant amounts of money.

Any assessment of these positions is inevitably polemic, for their basic premises suggest a highly oversimplified and unsophisticated approach to the political system. No given structural arrangement in itself is superior to another, but those advocating a change from bicameralism make just such a judgment, the validity of which is both unattested to and largely indeterminable. To identify "poor legislative output," unclear channels of responsibility, inefficiency, or any other allegedly undesirable characteristic with bicameralism and to fail to recognize the potential for these in a unicameral system is to pretend that structural arrangements cause such characteristics. While structural arrangements do have some effect, behavior patterns of politicians are the real stuff of politics, and to assume that unfavorable or undesirable behavior patterns can be eliminated by structural changes is to assert the unprovable. Indeed, careful study of the political system suggests that structural arrangements are largely a result rather than a determinant of the "politics" of the society; in other words, structural arrangements develop out of behavior patterns rather than vice versa. Thus it is incorrect to assume that bicameralism is undesirable because it produces certain patterns of undesirable behavior.

It is equally important to realize that the basic rationale for a bicameral system at the national level is inappropriate for the states. In the federal plan it was necessary to provide representation for preexisting units of government, the states, in such a way that their powers would not be seriously threatened either by the other members of the union or by the new national government itself. However, as we have already noted, in the case of the states all governing power belongs to them, and no other unit can claim inherent power. The cities and local governing units are subagents of the states, exercising state power. The powers of these local units are not protected against usurpation by the state because they are exercised only by leave of the state. Furthermore, protection of preexisting units of government is not the reason for two systems of representation in the state legislatures, for the simple reason that these units of government are created by the state.

In sum, the real justifications for two houses at the state level are familiarity and tradition. The test of desirability must be effectiveness, but its measure requires careful articulation of the values of the measurer. If, as in this volume, the premise is that a democratic process works well when there is an on-going, effective, open competition for political power, and when public policy results from the reconciliation of competing interests, then one may be forced to the conclusion that while there may be more "efficient" ways, in terms of economy of time, effort, and finances, to carry on the legislative function, one is hard pressed to find evidence that a bicameral legislature at the state level is more or less effective than a unicameral legislature would be. Our experience with unicameralism at this level is too limited to make such a judgment possible.

Below the state level there is mostly unicameralism. Before the twentieth century a great number of cities, particularly those with over 25,000 people, had bicameral city councils. At the beginning of this century about 30 percent of these cities still had bicameral legislatures. But one of the municipal reform movement's most notable successes was to abolish bicameralism so that local government is now unicameral.[2] Counties are governed by unicameral legislative bodies, and although the name varies, the structural arrangements are essentially the same throughout the United States. The legislative bodies of special districts are also uniformly unicameral.

One additional characteristic of the unicameral legislature of local governments is the frequency with which it also functions in an executive capacity. There is often no separation of powers between the executive and the legislature. County governing boards uniformly perform both legislative and executive functions, although as noted in Chapter 4, some counties have begun to hire chief executive officers or county managers. The usual pattern for special districts is for all functions to be performed by the elected or appointed board. In the cities only the traditional mayor-council form provides a clear distinction between the executive and legislature. Both the commission form (in which there are several commissioners serving collectively as a legislative body and individually as administrators of the various departments) and the council-manager form (in which the chief executive officer is hired and removed by the council) combine the executive and legislative functions in the legislative body.

Advocates of either of the systems must recognize that there is no evidence to suggest that either bicameralism or unicameralism is essential to proper representation in the democratic policymaking

[2] Some would consider New York City to be bicameral, in that it has a council elected by wards and, in addition, a Board of Estimate with an ex-officio membership. The Board reviews the budget prior to its submission to the council, and the council can only reduce or delete provisions from it. See Wallace S. Sayre and Herbert Kaufman, *Governing New York City* (New York: Russell Sage Foundation, 1960), p. 627.

process. Overemphasizing structural arrangements as the reason for desirable or undesirable political results has been a familiar error that needs to be replaced by close assessment of the evidence as to how the various structures actually operate as integral parts of the political subsystems.

Size of Legislative Bodies

There is absolutely no uniformity as to size of legislative bodies, and no judgments can be made about the relative merits of the various sizes. In the states, the upper house of the legislature has from 17 to 67 members and the lower house from 35 to 400.

The size of city councils varies from two members in a number of cases to 50 members in the Chicago city council. In general larger councils, while perhaps justified because they have an acceptable pattern of representation for a major city, has proved less efficient and effective than the smaller ones in deliberating and determining policy. In recent years there has been a trend toward smaller city councils. Mayor-council cities tend to have the larger councils, while those with a council-manager form have five to nine members, and the commission cities have predominantly five-member commissions.

The most common size for county governing bodies is three to five members, although cases exist where a single individual performs the function and others where the governing board is as large as 70 or 80. The usual range is from three to 50. Special districts are usually governed by a plural body of three, five, or seven members.

A search for a general principle on optimum size for legislative bodies is futile. There is no reliable evidence that any particular size directly affects the production of politically acceptable policy. On the other hand, within any particular subsystem a consideration of the effect of the legislature's size upon representativeness is entirely appropriate and desirable. A given legislative body may be too large or too small, not because it fails to meet some *a priori* standard as to optimum size but because it fails to meet the requirements of representativeness in the democratic policymaking process.

Membership: Selection, Terms, Compensation

State legislatures are in all cases composed of elected representatives of certain specified geographical areas. Until recently, the membership of the lower house was apportioned according to population and the upper house according to geographic area. Because of the recent reapportionment decisions of the Supreme Court, both houses of state legislatures must be apportioned on the basis of population.

Some states have already made the required change, and others are in the process of doing so.

Terms of office in state legislatures are usually two or four years, with the upper house generally having a longer term than the lower house. The majority of lower houses have two-year terms, and most of the upper houses have four-year terms. The legal requirements for election to state legislatures usually include United States citizenship, a prescribed length of time as a resident of the state and of the area from which elected, a specified age, and eligibility to vote. Compensation for state legislatures has been notoriously low in most instances, primarily because of the traditional view that it is a civic duty or an honor to serve and not a profession or profit-making activity. However, in recent years these views have changed somewhat, and while most states still have relatively small compensation, it has been increasing. At the upper limits are New York with $20,000 and California with $16,000. In addition, in some states rather significant expense allowances are added to this annual salary. However, the prevailing pattern is for the legislators' compensation to be significantly less than that of an executive or administrative officer and a good deal less than what the members could make as lawyers, doctors, farmers, or businessmen. Indeed, many states still do not consider the legislature as a full-time occupation, and compensate members for "inconveniences" incurred but not for their services.

At the local level, city council members are elected to terms generally ranging from one to six years, although the four-year term has become the norm. The tendency is to elect members at large, that is, without dividing the city into wards with a representative from each one. The larger cities, those over 500,000 population, tend to use the ward system. The method of selection—by ward or at large—is important insofar as it affects representation. Some argue that wards allow minority groups to have guaranteed representation on the city council (since wards often coincide with de facto segregated residential areas), but the record demonstrates that it is not difficult for dominant groups to gerrymander wards to avoid this result. Again, it can be seen that the structural arrangement itself is no guarantee of a particular result, good or bad. What the reader must do in considering the selection method in his own local area is to consider the *results* of the elections in terms of who is elected to the local governing unit and whose interests seem to be represented most effectively. Any attempt to formulate a generalized principle on a preferable system is likely to mislead one in evaluating the effectiveness of representation.

Compensation for city councilmen varies greatly. In small- and medium-sized cities they are paid little or nothing, apparently on the premise that it is a part-time job requiring more dedication and public spirit than time, with sufficient reward in the prestige and satisfaction in serving. Larger cities tend to pay larger salaries, and a few of the largest have salaries comparable to nongovernmental professions. Salaries tend to be smallest in council-manager cities, where the council usually has a smaller role to play than the professional manager, and highest in the few remaining commission governments, where the councilmen also serve as administrative heads of major departments.

County governing boards are almost invariably elected. Some few counties have elected members at large, but the prevalent pattern is for the members to be chosen from districts or other governmental subdivisions of the county. Most county boards are elected for four years, although some are elected for as long as eight years. Since these are part-time jobs, with a board meeting once or several times a month, compensation is usually minimal, from one hundred to several thousand dollars a year plus per diem or expense allowances. However, in some cases, such as Los Angeles County, the board of supervisors or the commissioners sit as a full-time body, and the compensation is substantial.

Special district boards defy generalization. The governing body may be appointed or elected, and the appointing authority may be the state, the city, the county, or any combination of these. Part or all of the membership may be ex officio, serving by virtue of the positions they hold in other capacities. Popular election of the board is generally the case in school districts, which account for the greatest percentage of special districts. However, in other types of districts popular election is not the general pattern, and special districts ordinarily are not closely connected to the electoral process. The boards are made up of persons known variously as commissioners, supervisors, trustees, directors, and are usually between three and five in number. They generally serve from two to six years. Both the county board and the special district board often function as the entire governing apparatus for their respective jurisdictions. They usually serve as the legislative and executive bodies, and some of the activities of a number of these boards are judicial in character.

Sessions

While most state legislatures convene only biennially, an increasing number, now twenty, have provided for annual sessions. There is also an evident trend toward longer legislative sessions, although most states still limit their length, most commonly to 60–90 days. Some of the larger states do not limit the length of the session, and others, while having constitutional limitations on length, use various subterfuges to allow the legislature to finish in the formally available time. The most popular technique is to "stop the clock," whereby the legislature pretends that as the legislative session approaches its prescribed limit the clock stops and does not start until business is completed. Another popular device is to adjourn at the prescribed time and to go immediately into special session. In most states the legislative activity is still considered a part-time occupation, and the traditional distrust of politicians is strong enough to sanction this belief. However, the press of business in the more heavily populated and highly industrial and urban states has increasingly demanded a more nearly full-time legislative body.

The usual pattern for city councils, county boards of supervisors, and the boards of special districts is occasional meetings to take care of the business of the jurisdiction. Some of the larger counties and cities now have full-time legislative bodies, but usually they meet only occasionally, such as once a month or when special business requires their meeting. Most special districts are very informally organized, and their boards meet only periodically. There is no formula as to how often a legislative body should meet, and no attempt should be made to devise one. Again the important task is to decide how effectively the legislative agency operates in the policymaking process, not how often or how long it meets.

Organization for Business

While there are variations most state legislatures follow the same general pattern of internal operation as the Congress of the United States—a decentralized committee system. At this point it becomes almost impossible to talk about city councils, county boards of supervisors, and the boards of special districts in a comparative fashion. These governing bodies are distinctly different from the state legislature in their internal operations primarily because they are not only legislative bodies but in most cases the major governing body of the jurisdiction. Hence their internal operations are not limited nor in many cases largely directed to the roles and functions of legislatures. Insofar as they perform those legislative functions they tend to do so without the highly formalized internal organization that is characteristic of state legislatures and Congress.

State legislatures operate largely through (1) a highly formalized power structure of legislative officials and (2) a highly formalized committee system. While there are various officials and employees in the legislative bodies—sergeants of arms, clerks, secretaries, typists— the most important official is the presiding officer of the lower house. This official, usually referred to as the Speaker, is nominally elected by the entire membership but in actual practice is selected by the majority party. The Speaker is elected from the membership of the lower house and has all the prerogatives of a member, but his most important powers are derived from his role as chairman and deter- miner of the distribution of time. He usually appoints all committee chairmen, and depending on the strength of party discipline in the legislature, he can force a considerable amount of party conformity on major policy questions. The upper house, the Senate, is usually presided over by the Lieutenant Governor who, as a nonmember of the body, generally has only titular powers.

Most of the substantive work of the legislature is done through its standing committees. The number varies, but there is usually one for each major area of legislation. While these committees are not miniature reproductions of the parent body, they usually represent fairly closely the distribution of political power in the parent body. These committees hold hearings, conduct debates, propose amend- ments, and make compromises; in short, they carry on the business of considering bills and proposals. It is in these committees that ac- cess by political interest groups is most crucial and productive. The whole house generally serves as a kind of final validating group for the work of the individual committees. Accommodation of conflicting interests can be made in the committees, and knowledgeable rep- resentatives of special interests recognize fully that their access to legislative committees is critical to their impact on the policymaking process. Obviously, who chairs these committees, who sits as mem- bers on them, and what political parties and interests they tend to favor, have an enormous impact on the product of the session.

In most cases, county boards of governors and city councils serve as their own committees; that is, public hearings are held directly before the governing body itself. However, in the larger cities and counties there is so much business that the governing body constitutes some members as subcommittees, which then hold public hearings. However, the system is not as highly institutionalized as it is in the state legislature, and the tradition is well established that the govern- ing body itself is the one before which all interested citizens should appear for a decision about public policy. In most special districts, with the major exception of school districts, the operations of the

governing boards are largely carried on without most residents of the
district paying any attention to them. Here, too, the board acts *en
banc* in considering policy matters.

Party and Politics

In Chapter 4 we noted the predominance of the two-party pattern
in state and local politics, though it is more prevalent in belief than
in practice. If, as we have contended, genuine competition for the
privilege of making public policy is at the heart of the democratic
process, then serious consideration should be given to the extent to
which that pattern continues after elections to affect the processes
for developing public policy. We argued that the main role of political parties is to serve as instruments for competition in elections,
but they also serve to continue the competition within government
among those who are privileged to make public policy. It is important
to recognize that a healthy, competitive interaction among various
interests is an important ingredient of the democratic policymaking
process.

Here the reader must be reminded that what he is seeking is an
understanding of the degree to which public policy emanating from
a legislative branch is in fact a reconciliation of competing interests
rather than the imposed policy of a dominant interest. In considering any given legislative arena, the key question is the effectiveness
of the competition between competing interests and of the processes
for reconciliation of those interests, not the existence or nonexistence
of a particular pattern of relationships.

Most state legislatures do not show strong, continuing intraparty
cohesion and discipline, nor do they demonstrate strong interparty
division. However, in some states control of the legislature is shifted
from one party to the other fairly frequently, whereas in others one
party tends to dominate for a long time. In some legislatures identification of continuing party positions is virtually impossible, whereas
in others consistent party-line voting is apparent. Legislative loyalties
seem to be tied to the constituency more frequently than to a party,
and divisions within the legislature tend more to be along an urban-
rural, conservative-liberal, labor-industry spectrum than along party
lines. However, though party discipline is often a nebulous ingredient
of the legislative process, party identification is almost universally
essential to the continuing electoral competition for political power.

County boards of governors and city councils are frequently nonpartisan, and the identification of political affiliation is difficult if not
impossible in these cases. (The problem of nonpartisanship was dis-

cussed in Chapter 4.) Here the reader must look behind formal relationships and structural arrangements to discover the actual patterns of political interaction and conflict, to determine the extent to which and the processes through which there is a representation of conflicting interests and a reconciliation of them in public policy. No generalization can substitute for such analysis. We began this chapter with a discussion of representation in public policy formation, suggesting that the policymaking arenas—here we concentrated on the legislative arena—can best be understood through an analysis of the ways in which they differ in terms of selection, access, and responsibility. The organizational and procedural aspects of legislatures in our state and local governments, which vary so much as to defy generalization, must be given careful consideration if one is to understand the roles of that legislative arena in the development of public policy.

Two Special Problems

Two special problems of importance warrant the attention of students of state and local government today. Both of them—reapportionment and the initiative—are at the heart of the problem of representation and the legislative function. Our consideration will be necessarily brief but may serve to focus much of the preceding discussion.

The Problem of Reapportionment

As the population has gradually but steadily shifted from rural areas to metropolitan, state legislatures have increasingly overrepresented rural areas. Most state leave to the legislature the responsibility for periodic reapportionment. However, most state legislatures ignore this responsibility, with the result that as population has shifted the representational base in the legislature has not. By 1960 only twenty-seven states had reapportioned within the last quarter century. Delaware had not reapportioned its legislature since 1897, Vermont since 1898, Alabama since 1901, and Connecticut since 1903. By 1960 it had become increasingly obvious that traditional remedies for the malapportionment of state legislatures were not adequate to meet the increasing demand of the urban areas for respresentation proportionate to their population. Many states were headed toward genuine crisis as the demands of the city, not just for representation but for solutions to its problems, were or seemed to be frustrated by such outdated apportionment.

By the 1950s it was clear in some states that the solution to this problem was not to come through traditional methods of reapportionment. It was equally clear that there was no alternative readily available to solve the problem. In 1946 the Supreme Court, in a suit involving an Illinois congressional district that had nine times as many constituents as any other district, refused to consider the case on its merits, holding that the question of legislative apportionment of the state was not within its jurisdiction.[3] Such questions were "political" questions, and in the opinion of Mr. Justice Frankfurter, "the courts ought not to enter into this political thicket." This (not unanticipated) reluctance of the Court to deal with such a question left those who were underrepresented in the state legislatures—and this was an increasing percentage of the population—with no apparent solution to their problem. Then, in a two-year period (1962–1964) the Supreme Court handed down what may be the most important series of decisions in this century. Certainly they are the most important ones affecting the distribution of political power in the states. In 1962, considering the contention of voters in Nashville, Tennessee that inequities in legislative districts denied them equal protection of the law under the Fourteenth Amendment, and noting that the Tennessee legislature had not been reapportioned in sixty years, the Court held that this apportionment question was not political and could be heard by federal courts, with the courts being empowered to develop a remedy when state legislatures failed to do so.[4]

While the court held only that the question of reapportionment of a state legislature was within the competence of a federal court to consider when there was an allegation that failure to apportion could deny equal protection of the laws, it quickly brought numerous challenges to existing apportionment in many states. In rapid succession the Supreme Court invalidated a Georgia county-unit system of representation, since it diluted the weight of some voters because of their place of residence;[5] suggested "one man, one vote" as the appropriate rule for voting in congressional elections, thus requiring that states bring their congressional districting up to date;[6] and required that representation in both houses of the state legislature must be according to population.[7]

Just what the final results of these monumental decisions will be is

[3] *Colegrove* v. *Green,* 328 U.S. 549.

[4] *Baker* v. *Carr,* 369 U.S. 186.

[5] *Gray* v. *Sanders,* 372 U.S. 368 (1963).

[6] *Wesberry* v. *Sanders,* 376 U.S. 1 (1964).

[7] *Reynolds* v. *Sims,* 377 U.S. 533 (1964).

difficult to predict. But there have already been certain changes. The Reynolds decision in effect told forty states that they had unconstitutional bases of representation in their state legislatures, and many of them have rapidly reapportioned their districts. Others have had their legislatures reapportioned under court-determined procedures, and still others are in the process of reapportioning. One thing is certain; now there is a solution to the disparity between residence and representation in the state legislature. Its impact on state politics can and probably will be great; rarely, if ever, in American history has a single set of decisions carried as much potential impact for the distribution of political power and for public policy. Indeed, the history of the reapportionment controversy in the next quarter century may show it to result in one of the most significant reevaluations of political processes and power ever witnessed in the United States. The shift of power to urban centers is almost inevitable; whether it will not bring with it problems as serious for the nonurban population as those felt by the urban population is by no means certain. The serious student of American government will find it imperative to follow the changing patterns of political power in our states as reapportionment proceeds.[8]

The Problem of the Initiative

The initiative, through which the people may legislate without action by the legislature, dates back to 1898, when South Dakota became the first state to provide for it. It was as a result of the Progressive Movement that the instruments of "direct democracy"— the initiative, referendum, and recall—were enacted into law in a number of states. Within the historical, ideological, and theoretical context of the first decade of the twentieth century this trilogy was advanced as a means of involving "the people," as opposed to "the interests," in public policymaking. Twenty states, mostly in the West, adopted the initiative at the state level, but no state has done so within the last forty years. Many states allow local use of the initiative, and it is available in some cities in almost every state.

While provisions vary, there have been three kinds of initiatives—

[8] The question of the applicability of the "one-man, one-vote" rule to other governmental agencies or units, especially counties, cities, and special districts, is of increasing concern in the courts. While no definitive answer can be given at this time, a thorough review of the decisions bearing on this question may be found in *United States Supreme Court Reports,* 18 L ed 2d 1537, reviewing both lower federal and United States Supreme Court cases. That the rule will eventually be applied generally to local governmental units appears likely.

the constitutional, the direct statutory, and the indirect statutory. The constitutional and direct statutory initiatives allow the electorate to make changes directly in the law of the state; the indirect initiative has been used to suggest legislative action demanded by the voters, usually with the proviso that if the legislature does not enact the measure it will become law without such action or will be submitted to the electorate at the next election. The constitutional initiative allows the electorate to amend the constitution. The direct statutory initiative permits the electorate to enact statutes directly without recourse to the legislature. The procedures for both are quite similar. First, those interested in placing an initiative on the ballot must draw up the proposal and submit it to a state official for authentication. Proponents must then circulate a petition for the signature of qualified voters. When the required number of signatures has been verified, the measure goes on the ballot, and if approved by a specified majority, it becomes law.

The initiative tends to be a "sacred cow" since its emphasis is on the role of the people in deciding public policy. Anyone who challenges it might be accused of not believing in public participation in policymaking.

Insofar as lawmaking is an integral part of policymaking, it is important to recognize that rarely if ever is public policy, or law, a reflection of an objective or "right" answer to a question of what government shall or shall not do. Experienced legislators know that rarely is legislating a simple process of choosing the right from the wrong policy. Major policy questions simply connot be simplified into a "yes" or "no" proposition. The legislative product is a result of conflict, compromise, reconciliation of interests, and the give and take of political dealing and manipulation necessary to draw together the required number of votes to pass the measure. This is the reason the most significant part of the legislative process occurs in committee, where those interested in the measure compete with others of differing interests in an effort to emerge with the maximum gain possible for each. The final vote on the floor, when the question is put, may appear to a novice to be a decision, but in reality it is a final affirmation and formalization of decisions already made in committee and conference rooms.

The real problem with the initiative is that it is not a good policymaking tool or technique. Its utilization is based on the failure to recognize the legitimate, indispensable role of conflict of interests. Before an initiative vote in an election can be meaningful the major decisions must have already been made; the choice must have been narrowed down to a "yes" or "no" on a given question. This means, of course, that the really difficult decisions must have been made prior to the time the question is submitted to the electorate. Elections, in short, are not policymaking instruments; at best they are instruments for determining the acceptability to the electorate of alternative policies or choices. The electorate can do little or nothing to determine the content of those alternatives. However, it is precisely this process for determining the alternatives presented to the electorate—the legislative process—that is the significant part of public policymaking. Submitting a proposition to the electorate as an initiative substitutes for this process; a pretense is made (one all too widely believed) that this is the correct way to make policy decisions.

Quite contrary to the belief that the initiative eliminates the power of special interests (which are apparently thought to operate too freely in influencing representatives in the legislature), the initiative allows a disproportionate weight to go to these established special interests. It allows those with sufficient money, professional public relations techniques, and inclination to determine without interference from "political dealing and compromising" what the content of a given policy alternative should be, to submit it in its *finished* form to the electorate without the necessity of reconciling all the interests concerned with such a policy. The result is that the electorate is asked to make a final decision on a proposition prior to the complex, continuing, and indispensable conflict of interests that should precede the formalization of policy. *In an initiative, policy is determined prior to the conflict over its nature.* There is no opportunity for compromise, for balancing interests, for amendment to accommodate conflict. This is not policymaking by the people, but a facade through which the very political interests feared in the legislative process are able to bypass the legitimate conflict there and ask the electorate to legitimize privately written legislation.

We fully recognize that the analysis presented here is at odds with many other textbook writers on American state and local government, for often it is said that direct legislation "can make truly significant contributions to state and local government." The potential may be there, but the reader should seriously consider that the initiative procedure may be inconsistent with a realistic theory of democracy.

6

Policymaking Arenas:
The Executive and Administrator

In Chapter 1 it was noted that the segmental study of the individual parts of a political system—the legislature, executives and administrators, and the courts—though necessary, is nevertheless misleading because it fails to demonstrate how the parts are related. No one part of an operating system can be separated from the whole without distortion of both. It is with this understanding that we proceed to the second major policymaking arena—the executive and administrator—and study it separately but with a view to understanding its relationships to other governmental units.

Some General Observations

Our consideration of state and local executives and administrators in policymaking is founded on three important observations. First, we must recognize that these executives-administrators are both policymakers and policy executors. Traditionally, we have viewed the executive as only an implementor, responsible for carrying out the law, and administrators as pseudoneutral but technically competent assistants to the executive. A more sophisticated understanding of their roles views them both as developers and major contributors to the making of policy, and as executors and administrators of developed policy. Indeed, to carry out successfully the second of these roles involves the first. Thus, the relationship of the executive-administrative with the legislative role must be understood if one is to understand the functioning of the state and local subsystems. Furthermore, when we consider local executives and administrators, the admixture of executive-administrative-legislative activities makes dissection impossible. At the local level, in city councils, county boards of supervisors or commissioners, and the governing bodies of special districts, the executive-administrative-legislative arenas are quite often identical. It is inappropriate to consider executives and administrators as nonpolicymaking agents.

A second important observation is that in tracing the development of the executive-administrative branch in American state and local government one can identify a continuing distrust of the executive. Indeed, one of the most persistent ingredients of American political temperament has been the fear of a strong executive. Historically, the legislature has been the stronger branch; early state governors were chosen by the legislature for very short terms, usually one year. Throughout most of the nineteenth century the governor was only the titular head of the state government, but by the first quarter of the present century there had been significant changes toward making the governor more powerful. One of the most notable successes of the reform movement at that time was the strengthening of the state executives, while paradoxically one of its successes at the local level was the weakening of the then-dominant political boss, the mayor. Since then the chief executive of the state has steadily gained power, but it would be misleading to conclude his is at all comparable to the power of the President. He does not dominate the government as does the President, even though he is in almost every case the most powerful and important state officeholder. The fear of a strong executive is manifested today in the position that local executives hold; the day of the all-powerful, dominating political figure in county or city government has long since past. The few remaining political "bosses," alluded to in Chapter 4, are clearly the exceptions.

The third observation, perhaps a corollary of the historic position of the weak executive, is that state and local governments generally evidence a lack of integrated executive-administrative power. The majority of the states and the overwhelming majority of local governments are characterized by a diffusion of political power. Few governors and even fewer mayors (commission executives and city managers are a special case) can boast of genuine administrative control of the vast complex of agencies making up the executive branch. Typically, the governor or the local executive is the titular head of these highly uncoordinated and irrationally structured offices and agencies. Largely beyond any effective control by the governor or mayor, some of these agencies fall within the jurisdiction of independently elected officials, others are administered by collegial bodies or administrators sometimes formally appointed by the executive and sometimes not. The widespread adoption of merit system or civil service procedures has also contributed to this lack of executive control by removing many patronage positions. At the state level another reason for this diffusion of power is the fact that few governors have any effective law-enforcing agency at their disposal. In most states, law enforcement and prosecution for crimes depends largely on locally selected officials. And the day when the mayor dominated the police force has passed in most states; today police forces are professional and in many cases operate under a rigid civil service system, largely independent of the executive. These factors—too many administrative agencies, popular election of a number of executives with division of power among them, an historical aversion to a strong executive, removal of the power of patronage, and the decentralization and professionalization of law-enforcing activities—indicate why many state governors and chief executives of major cities, legally charged with responsibility for directing and supervising government, are legally incompetent to do so effectively.

Roles of the Governor

No simple explanation is possible of what it means to be a governor. The governor is part of an institution; separating the individual, the governor, from the institution, the governorship, is usually impossible. While the successful governor most often appears to the voters to be doing the job all alone, in reality he is part of a much larger and more significant entourage of which he may or may not be the central figure. The governorship is made up of the governor himself, his personal and official staff, often other elected officials, frequently major administrative officers, and usually important political personalities who may or may not hold public office. While no one person could do the job alone, political success demands that he appear to, and tradition has it that he alone bears full responsibility—and the consequent political cost or benefit—for success or failure of the state's executive function.

No uniform list of executive powers can be drawn up for all fifty states, but the following are the usual ones: fiscal control through preparation of the budget which outlines anticipated revenue needs and expenditures; appointment or removal of administrative and judicial officials; veto power over legislative acts (and in many states an item veto over individual appropriations in general appropriation acts); clemency powers (commutations, pardons, and paroles); military powers, as commander in chief of the state's militia; and political leadership as titular head of his party and as the most successful politician at the state level. These powers can best be understood not through a consideration of the variety of legal details bearing upon them in the fifty states but through a consideration of the major roles played by the governor in making and executing policy. These roles are: (1) chief of state; (2) chief executive and administrator; (3) political leader; (4) chief legislator or legislative advocate; (5) commander-in-chief of the state militia; and (6) quasi-judicial activities.

Chief of State

The ceremonial role of the chief executive is far more important than some of his more formal roles. As chief of state the governor personifies the government. To many people in the state he is government and authority. He is responsibile for everything good and most of the bad. It is the governor who does or fails to do things, who imposes taxes and expands services. He must greet visitors, dedicate new highways, ceremonially ascend to the top of new buildings, issue formal statements upon the death of prominent citizens, pin awards on visiting dignitaries, crown beauty queens, affectionately pat the hindquarter of prize bulls at the state fair—in short, he must be visible at a host of public occasions and verbal at many more. He also formally represents the state in meetings with executives of other states, with federal officials, and in some cases, with officials from other nations. This visibility of the governor is a most critical factor in making the tremendously complex and impersonal thing called "government" identifiable and acceptable to the citizen.

It would be extremely difficult to verify or demonstrate empirically just what is involved in performing this ceremonial function, but experienced observers and participants in state politics all testify to its tremendous importance. It is important not only in terms of identifying government, of personifying and personalizing the highly impersonal business of governing, but also in terms of the political exposure it provides for the governor. The drain on the governor's energies and time in this function is compensated for by the political gain for him in performing it. Through such public exposure the governor has continuing contact with actual and potential voters. This is important not only in terms of the support it may give him and his administration in developing policy, in relating to the legislature, and in directing the administrators, but also in terms of his need to develop strength in the competition for political power between elections.

Chief Executive and Administrator

While many citizens look to the governor as the personification of the state, they likewise expect him to be the actual chief executive and controller of the administration. In principle this is the case; the governor is the chief executive and administrative officer, and he is responsible for directing the vast administrative complex that is today's state government. This view is supported by popular myth, but few governors can actually preform this role.

In most states the governor lacks the legal power to exercise executive direction of the government. Usually he has to share his power with other executives and administrators. First, there are often several elected state officials, such as the lieutenant governor, secretary of state, treasurer, attorney general, auditor, and sometimes superintendent of public instruction, who have both independent political power by virtue of their own electoral status and legal responsibility and powers quite apart from those of the governor. Second, there is usually a large number, not uncommonly more than a hundred and in a few cases, such as California, over three hundred, of administrative departments, boards, commissions, officials, or agencies, making up the executive or administrative branch that have little or no coordination among them or with the governor's office. Third, these agencies, including some having departmental status, are often headed by officials whose terms of office do not coincide with the governor's, or they are made up of members serving overlapping terms so that the governor can fill only a few of the positions. In some states major administrative agencies are composed of personnel selected by the legislature.

The lack of an integrated administrative branch, the multiplicity of agencies, and their variety of composition, all increase the governor's difficulty in exercising administrative control. Most symptomatic of this difficulty is the general restriction on the governor in filling positions. While most governors still have a rather large number of appointments they may or are required to make, in very few states is the governor now in a position to shape an administration through his appointive power. Most of the important activities of government are in one way or another independent of the governor's appointive power. He obviously cannot fill the most important positions when they are elective. He cannot control departments headed by such officials, unless he and the other elected officials have a particularly close political bond. In many cases even when he is authorized to fill vacancies his appointments must be approved by the legislature. Even though in many states the governor still appoints a great variety of subordinate officers, in most cases this does not seem to increase his power materially over administrative agencies. Indeed, the day of patronage (filling governmental positions with political friends to reward faithful political service) is largely at an end. Civil service and merit systems, though not universally adopted, have cut further into the control the governor may have over the administration through the appointive procedures.

Even more restricted is the governor's power to remove officials. Most states do not grant the governor a general power here. In most cases the governor can remove those officials whom he appoints only "for cause." In some cases these are subject to senatorial approval. Many officials are simply beyond the governor's removal authority by virtue of their being elected. A further limitation on the governor's power to remove officials is political; governors often find that wholesale removal of officials or even selective removal of a given official, though legally possible, is politically undesirable either because of the independent political support of the officials or because of the ammunition such actions may give to actual or potential opponents. Although some governors may become strong and effective executives and chief administrators, they usually do so in spite of their legal position.

Control of the budget can be an important mechanism for administrative control, but though many states have made significant strides toward implementing an executive budget, the control that a typical governor can exercise over independent agencies through the budget still leaves much to be desired for effective executive direction. However, this curtailment of the governor's power to direct administrative agencies is not viewed as an undesirable situation, having come about in response to public demands that governors not be allowed to become too strong and that many activities be insulated from "political" control by the governor.

Political Leader

In most states the governor is at least titular head of his political party. However, his power in the party may be more apparent than real. Some governors are in fact the most important political figure in the state, effective leaders of their parties, dispensers and determiners of political favor. On the other hand, some governors are simply figureheads for the real political leadership, selected and elected by political "bosses" to perpetuate a political lineage. The position of most governors is somewhere between these two extremes; they are recognized as the leaders of their parties, they influence its activities, but they do not dominate it or its influential leaders. The variety of governor-party relationships is too numerous to permit generalization or categorization, but recognizing the important aspects of that relationship will help the reader to analyze the governor of his own state as a party leader.

Some of the questions that need to be answered to assess the governor's position as a political leader are: Is he recognized generally, not only by the average citizen but by influential politicians, as the leader of his party? Does he select the party chairman, not just in name but in fact? Is he consulted on questions of major party position or platform stance? Is it he or his entourage who determines the candidates for other positions on the party slate? Does he have a major role in nominating candidates? Does he or his advisor direct the party's campaign tactics? Does he head a slate of officials under the party designation at election time? Does he control or influence the use of party finances? To what extent is he able to reward party members by appointment to public office? Can he "punish" recalcitrant members of his own political party? Does he have solid relationships with local politicos? Is he identified with the dominant wing or faction of his party? Does he have major influence with the legislature?

Obviously it is an extremely difficult task to assess the political leadership of the governor. Much depends upon factors having little or nothing to do with his personality, competence, or ambition. Party organization, the tradition of two-party competition or intraparty factional disputes, legal and institutional limitations on his power, social and economic conditions, and a host of other factors may prevent effective leadership. Another very important consideration here may be the position of the state in national politics. For instance, a governor of one of the large, populous states with a large number of electoral votes is almost automatically a potential presidential or vice presidential candidate by virtue of the state's importance in the presidential election. Thus the governor of California or New York may have important political influence within the state that is almost entirely based on his importance in national politics.

In most states the governor is at least the most visible political leader, and in many he is the most important political figure. His role as a party and political leader is, of course, inevitably intertwined and admixed with everything else he does as governor.

The Governor as Legislator

It is in the legislature as a leader in making policy that the governor comes into his own. In most states he is the chief legislator, having significant powers to guide and direct the legislature to adopt policy positions he determines or suggests. In Chapter 5 it was noted that while lawmaking may be the most obvious role of a legislative body, particularly of the state legislature, such a body performs its most important roles in informing the electorate, in reconciling competing interests, and in legitimizing policy decisions made elsewhere. It is in the last role that the relative power of the governor to determine policy can be seen. It is increasingly common for the legislature to validate and legitimize policy suggested by the governor. As a result, the most familiar power of the legislature has become a negative one, the power to delay, modify, and even obstruct decisions.

The reasons for the governor's importance in legislation are not hard to detect. The most important lies in the nature of the legislature. It is made up of individuals representing parts of the state. Its provincialism is inherent in its structure, and its members' interests tend to be directed to their own constituencies rather than to broader matters. Since the legislator's constituency determines the interests he will represent, the fragmentation of constituencies in the legislature promotes fragmentation of interests. On the other hand, the governor's constituency is state-wide, and the matters he finds most profitable to support tend to be those that have greatest appeal to the state-wide electorate.

This difference in representational base helps to explain the legislature's customary slowness to adopt new or radical programs. While partly due to its collegial nature, its lack of aggressive leaders who are closely attuned to the demands of a state-wide electorate and the narrow scope of demands placed on legislators by their (until recently) mostly rural constituents better explains its lethargy. A governor, on the other hand, must compete for a state-wide constituency; his electorate is a composite of the electorates of all the legislators. Although certain areas of the state are more important in terms of their electoral strength, the governor must align himself with concerns and interests over the whole state, and he can appeal to these more effectively than can the representative of a small provincial area. When the governor advocates state-wide programs he speaks to the concerns of the electorate for which he competes. Obviously, his position and power in his party relative to individual leaders of the legislature are important in determining just how effective he may be in legislative leadership, but his ability to appeal to the state's electorate may help to develop his relative position as a party leader.

Another explanation of the important role of the governor in legislative policy involves the tools available to him. One of these is particularly related to his state-wide constituency—his ability to call attention to policy questions through messages to the legislature and public addresses. Messages to the legislature allow him to inform it of needed policy considerations, and in providing such messages he can direct the attention of not only the legislators but also the general public to questions he finds desirable (and, of course, politically profitable for himself). As the most visible state official he also has at his disposal much of the newsmaking and -reporting machinery in the state. Thus by scheduling speeches, visits, or otherwise "making news," he may gain headlines in a way considerably more productive of public notice than an individual legislator could. This public relations role of the governor might well be listed as a separate one, except that it is threaded through all his roles. It is, however, perhaps most noticeable in his relationship with the legislature.

The role of the governor as chief administrator gives him considerable influence in the legislative process because of the administrators' dependence on him in their apparent if not actual conflict with the legislature over appropriations, approval and supervision of programs, and because of the general role of the legislature to oversee the administrative branch. The governor can generally obtain support from administrative agencies, at least insofar as his proposals do not run counter to their interests, and he can call on them to provide the data and testimony necessary to get proposals through the legislature. When the governor aligns himself with the administrators, or vice versa, the legislature is likely to be a rather disadvantaged opponent. Of course, occassionally the legislature is able to align itself with the administrators, but the lack of a recognized authority figure in the legislature mitigates against this. Furthermore, insofar as the governor has appointive and removal powers over the agencies, he may use such power as an actual or implied lever to achieve cooperation.

Executive-appointed commissions or study groups relate the governor and the legislature in still another way. Composed of leading citizens, academic authorities, members of the governor's entourage, support groups, and quite often, potentially hostile members of the opposition, they focus public attention on a particular policy of the governor's choosing, highlighting a question that otherwise might receive little or no consideration by the legislature. Often the prestige of such groups and the public tendency to ascribe expertise to their findings lend support to the governor's policy directions in a fashion difficult to duplicate or counter in the legislature.

It is here that the budgetary power of the governor is important. Most states use an executive budget system in which the governor proposes expenditures and revenue sources for a year, and after the legislature has enacted the budget, he oversees expenditures of the administrative agencies. Although in many states this system is not as effective for executive control as at the national level, the budget is a major policy statement, and insofar as the legislature is required or invited to consider the appropriations the governor suggests it is thus directed to consider the policy questions he has outlined. While most legislatures will make significant changes in his budget suggestions, in most cases the budget message, its proposals, and the appropriation bills arising from it make up the most significant segment of the legislature's work during any given session.

The veto and the control over special sessions are important formal tools the governor holds to check the legislature. All states except North Carolina give the governor the power to veto legislation. Usually, however, the veto is only a final resort after all other measures for influencing the legislative output are undertaken. A threat of veto may induce the legislature to comply with gubernatorial wishes. Forty-two states give the governor the item veto, which enables him to disapprove individual items in an appropriation act. In at least one case (Washington) the item veto extends to measures other than appropriations acts. Obviously, the governor's ability to influence legislation, and his ability to influence individual legislators, is greatly increased by his actual or potential use of the veto. The evidence suggests that the governor's veto power often can induce legislative response in keeping with his policy preferences.

All states allow the governor to call special sessions of the legislature, and in many states such sessions are restricted to considering only those measures included in the governor's call. Thus, through a special session, the governor may gain public exposure for his own programs, or by threatening such a session he may coerce the legislators, particularly in an election year when they may be anxious to get back to their districts to campaign.

Commander in Chief

Traditionally, the governor has been the commander in chief of state military forces. The militia, or National Guard, is subject to his command in every state unless and until it is taken into national service by the President. In recent years the Guard has been used increasingly as a means of putting down civil disturbances in the major cities. Supporters of the Guard, always politically effective in protecting it, now find renewed strength in their demands for a strong state militia to cope with actual or potential disturbances associated with racial tensions in metropolitan areas. The Guard also is available in cases of disaster, such as tornadoes, hurricanes, floods, forest fires, and in most states it is an integral part of the civil defense program.

On occasion the National Guard can be used as a direct instrument of a governor's political policy. For instance, in 1934, Governor Huey

Long of Louisiana used the militia to seize voting lists in New Orleans to avoid defeat of his political machine at the polls. More recently, in 1957, Governor Orville Faubus of Arkansas used the National Guard to block the implementation of federal orders desegregating a high school in Little Rock. Subsequently President Eisenhower federalized the Arkansas National Guard, thus removing it from the governor's control. Again in 1962 and 1963, in Mississippi and Alabama President Kennedy federalized the National Guard to remove it as an instrument of the governors' opposition to desegregation orders. The military power of the state's chief executive is more apparent than real today, and his exercise of it is severely limited both politically and jurisdictionally.

Judicial Activities

There is a category of executive powers or roles that for lack of a better term is usually referred to as judicial or quasi-judicial but that might be more accurately described as clemency. A recognized part of the judicial process of every state is the executive role in commuting sentences, granting reprieves and pardons, and approving parole for convicted law violators. While the specific procedures vary, the legal responsibility for granting such clemency is usually vested in the governor, with the concurrence of some agency of which the governor may or may not be a member also frequently required. In years past governors of some states have exercised this clemency power freely, but today the political disadvantages from its unwise use are potentially so great as to mitigate against its use at all. Increasingly the states are providing for some agency to act upon such matters, either through advice to the governor or binding recommendations to him.

Rendition of fugitives, often referred to as extradition, is also a role of the governor. The Constitution obligates the states to return fugitives to a state from which they flee. This "rendition clause," [1] while apparently mandatory in its provisions, has been interpreted by the Supreme Court [2] to impose only a moral duty on the governor, one that there is no political or legal force to sanction. Most governors usually routinely honor extradition requests from their fellow governors, but an increasing number of states provide an administrative procedure for investigating the circumstances and advising the governor on rendition. Such a procedure accomplishes two things: it seems to increase the probability that justice will be done, that

[1] Article IV, Section 2.
[2] *Kentucky* v. *Dennison,* 24 Howard 66 (1861).

fugitives will be rendered up only in the interest of justice, and it tends to insulate the governors from political ramifications of an incorrect decision.

The governor's most profound effect on the judicial process in the state may be through his power of appointment to the judiciary. Insofar as he is the one who selects those who will sit on the bench he will have a significant impact on the character of that bench. However, in many states this role has been substantially circumscribed by provision for popular election of many judges and by various administrative procedures whereby the appointments are to be made only from panels specifically authenticated by some type of judicial appointment commission.

In summary, the governor is by far the most important official in state government. The roles discussed above make him potentially and in most cases actually the most powerful individual in the state. The combination of his ceremonial, executive, political, legislative, military, and judicial powers makes it possible for him to affect the political lives of other governmental officials and makes him potentially extremely important in making and implementing policy. That some governors have been comparatively impotent reflects an inability to maximize potential strength, but such instances are comparatively infrequent. Even our historic fear of a strong executive, the lack of an integrated executive-administrative system, and the existence, in some states, of rival executives independently elected and functioning with separate power—even these do not change the fact that in most states the governor is both the personification of government and the repository of a large share of governmental power.

Local Executives

Counties and special districts are usually governed by a collegial body, a board of supervisors or commissioners, police jury, or some other multiple-membered body that serves as both the legislature and executive. There is usually no executive officer as such, although there may be a chairman of the board and, in some few cases, a county may have a chief administrative officer, county manager, or a county mayor. However, the executive function is usually the responsibility of the entire county or special district board. A large proportion of cities also operate without separation into executive and legislative branches. Cities organized into a commission form of government (in which there is a collegial body serving as both the legislature and collective executive, with each member or commissioner being responsible for a major administrative activity of the city) combine not only executive-legislative powers in the strict sense but also place responsibility for the day-to-day administrative activity of the city on the same group. While the use of a commission form of government has been decreasing in recent years, there has been a steady and continual increase in the number of cities operating under a council-manager, in which the city council, serving as the legislature and the executive, hires a city manager to be the chief administrative officer. Here, in what is the most popular modification of local government in this century, there is a combination of legislative and executive-administrative responsibility in one body.

In only one important and generally used form of local government is there a clear division between executive and legislative power. This is in the mayor-council form, in which there is an independently elected mayor and council each exercising its respective functions. This is the most popular form of city government in the United States. (The same separation is present in a limited number of counties, which have an independently elected county mayor.)

Even in this form of government, however, the power of the mayor may vary significantly. Political scientists are fond of distinguishing between weak and strong mayor-council forms of government. The distinction is based on the possession of administrative power by the mayor. If the mayor is able to appoint and remove administrative officers, and thus control or dominate the administrative structure, political scientists tend to designate him as a strong mayor. In the absence of such administrative power, even though the mayor possesses a veto power over the council, he would be designated a weak mayor. In most cases there is no significant difference between a weak and strong mayor in his relationship to the council. The strong mayor, though, has important and significant powers over the administrative agencies and agents of the city. Particularly important is his budgetary power. When he has control over the preparation of the budget and over the expenditure of funds, he is well on his way to significant administrative power. In a weak mayor-council system, the council generally has more significant relationships with administrative offices than does the mayor. Several important administrators may be appointed by the council, and the mayor is usually prohibited from removing administrative officials without the council's acquiescence. Budgetary control is generally beyond the authority of the mayor. There also may be a rather long list of popularly elected city officials. However, even if the mayor is "weak," he is not often excluded from important policymaking activities. As Charles Adrian says, "The mayor is not 'weak' because he lacks policymaking power—he normally has a veto, can recommend legislation, and may even preside over the council. He is 'weak' because he lacks administrative power." [3] In fact, some mayors of comparatively weak administrative power have been noted for being extremely effective in influencing the development of policy. However, we would anticipate that an executive who does not have administrative powers would be significantly less effective in influencing policy.

It is apparent that the first of our three observations at the beginning of this chapter is applicable to local executives—executive-administrative officials are also policymakers. The combination of executive and legislative powers in the same officials in our counties, special districts, commission and council-manager cities clearly suggests that local executives can be expected to play significant roles in policymaking.

Many observers conclude that the second observation—distrust of the executive in the American political temperament—must be limited largely to state executives. But the evidence is subject to different interpretations. The widespread use of combined executive and legislative power and the relatively limited use of strong executives, for example, does not support this conclusion. The fact that the executive and legislative powers are combined at the county level, the special district level, and the experimentation with the commission form of government and the enthusiasm for the council-manager form might all be said to support the opposite point of view. Furthermore, a rather widespread incidence of the "weak" as opposed to the limited use of the "strong" mayor in the mayor-council form of government might further support the opposition. On the other hand, American local government is historically identified with extremely strong mayors in many parts of the country. The domination of most of the major cities in the early part of the nineteenth century by strong political bosses is a matter of record.

Perhaps a better explanation of what has been occurring in recent years to the executive in local government would not be couched in terms of fear of the executive but instead in terms of high regard for professionalism and competence. Thus local government is more responsive to demands for organizational patterns that develop administrative and executive competence rather than to a fear of a strong executive. In any case, the result is virtually the same—both at the state and the local level there are very few all-powerful, dominating

[3] *Governing Urban America* (New York: McGraw-Hill Book Company, Inc., 1961), p. 201.

political figures. Particularly at the local level the executive is not the controlling agency of government.

The third general observation made earlier about the lack of integrated executive-administrative power appears to be almost paradoxical with the combination of executive-legislative power. Nonetheless, in the overwhelming majority of local governments there is a diffusion of political power. Few local executives have genuine administrative control and supervision of the complex of agencies in the city government. In the counties, special districts, and in most of the cities, even in these with "strong" mayors, there is no one executive who has effective administrative control over the agencies of government. The discussion of this lack of integration of executives and administrative power in the first part of this chapter seems to be applicable to almost all local governments.

It is worth noting that there are many kinds of executive and administrative officers in most local communities. Some of these are elected, others appointed. There is likely to be a clerk, a city attorney or county counsel, several elected department heads, a treasurer, a controller, an auditor, and an assessor. The police chief and the fire chief may be elected. There is also apt to be a city engineer and a county engineer, and a city and county planner. Whether or not these lesser executive officials are elected or appointed, they share executive-administrative power with the chief executive when there is one, and with the legislature and executive in most counties, special districts, and commission and manager forms of city government. This diffusion of executive-administrative powers is one of the most significant aspects of local government in the United States.

7

Policymaking Arenas: The Judiciary

The courts make policy, but a large proportion of the American people either do not know or prefer not to recognize this. Popularly the courts are considered as nonpolitical agencies engaged only in adjudicating conflicts and interpreting the applicability of law. But they are an integral part of the policymaking process, an important arena for conflict, and their roles in adjudication of conflicts and interpretation of the applicability of laws are part of that process. This chapter seeks to explain this approach to the study of the courts and to aid the reader to examine his own state courts to discover their contribution to the political process.

Some Important Observations

Our consideration of state courts as part of the policymaking process will be made clearer by five observations about the nature of the judicial process.

Political Character of Courts

No fiction is more firmly established in American governmental folklore than that the courts are nonpolitical, that they do not make policy, that they simply interpret the law. This, however, is not a realistic view of the judiciary at any level. Much of the work of the courts is to adjudicate conflicts arising over specific application of legal requirements, but this often involves clarification of the meaning of a statute or other policy pronouncement, and this in turn involves definition or redefinition of public policy. In constitutional interpretation the courts determine the definitive meaning of constitutional provisions and thus establish the framework in which other policymakers must operate.

One must guard against distortion by overstatement, however. Most of the business of the courts involves public policymaking only in an incidental fashion. Generally the public's contact is with the lower level courts which handle thousands of cases, few of which make policy. Traffic cases, small claims, misdemeanors, felonies, and probate make up a large percentage of these. Most cases flow from the application of state and local laws that affect people's daily lives. These cases may be tremendously important for the individuals involved, but in most cases it is an overstatement to argue that they are of serious general import in developing or changing public policy. Furthermore, the courts depend largely upon other agencies of government to direct their activities and to provide the legislation and the ordinances that result in legal actions. Thus the potential impact of their determinations on broad-scale public policy has already been circumscribed by the nature of the instruments with which they are asked to deal. Nevertheless, most students of the courts agree that they do have important policymaking roles. In fact, even their "ordinary" cases, dealing with enforcement of established legal norms, may have serious repercussions in determining who benefits, and in what ways, from participation in the political system.

Furthermore, the nonpolitical character of state courts is illusionary from the standpoint of their selection. The selection of members to sit on state courts is very much a part of the political process, affected by and affecting political relationships with other officials. Most state courts have elected justices, but even here the myth is popular, reflecting a refusal to recognize the impossibility of having elections without politics. Appointment by political leaders is no less political because there is no nonpolitical way to choose people who by their selection affect the political lives of those doing the choosing. But the myth survives, and its strength is attested to not only by its persistent repetition by layman, lawyer, and scholar alike but also by the vehemence with which the courts are criticized when they obviously step into political character.

One of the best summaries of this topic has been contributed by a leading scholar of the state courts, Kenneth N. Vines, who concludes

that the politics of the judiciary is similar in many ways to politics elsewhere in the political system. . . . that courts are involved in partisan activities and are responsive to interest demands; that although much of what they do is routine, they are sometimes involved in political controversies of great passion; and judges interact in patterns of conflict and consensus and are influenced by many of the same social and economic forces that move other political actors. Moreover, the organization and staffing of the courts reflect long-standing political traditions or else serve various political needs.[1]

The following discussion subscribes to Vines's view that while this legal myth may serve important social purposes a realistic view of the political functions of the courts better informs us of their nature and problems. The myth cannot be overlooked since it is the way the public perceives the courts, but it should not be a substitute for an accurate description of the way the courts operate as a part of the political system.

Public Acceptance and Support

The courts enjoy a comparatively high level of public acceptance and support. Their perceived nonpolitical character, the sparsity of information about the way they operate, and the infrequency of public contact with them help to explain their comparative immunity from challenge and the willingness of citizens to acquiesce in judicial determinations with little dissatisfaction (until the courts are thought to be handing down "political" decisions). While there is little reluctance to criticize the legislature, the governor, and other political figures, there is significantly more tolerance of the operations of the courts and of judicial officials. Despite vocal opponents of the courts, and periods of rather widespread disillusionment with them, their immunity from such forces is significantly greater than that of the other governmental branches.

One important consequence (or perhaps cause) of this set of circumstances has been a failure to examine the courts in the detail and with the thoroughness with which legislative and executive agencies have been examined. We know much less about the judicial arena than about the others. The decisionmaking process in the courts is little studied primarily because scholars are not welcome there; we are only now beginning systematic research on state courts. This insulation from inspection has been reinforced by an aura of inviolability. The scholar who suggests that courts can and should be studied systematically to discover how they operate is looked upon with apprehension that he might change them in the process. It cannot be denied that such a danger exists, for demonstrating the inappropriate-

[1] "Courts as Political and Governmental Agencies," in Herbert Jacob and Kenneth N. Vines (eds.), *Politics in the American States: A Comparative Analysis* (Boston: Little, Brown and Company, 1965), p. 283.

ness of a popular myth may in fact change the institution around which that myth is built.

Dual System of Courts

There is a complex dual system of courts in the United States. Not only is there a distinctive federal court system—made up of the Supreme Court, the Courts of Appeal, and the federal district courts —but also there is a wide variety of state courts systems. Law is essentially either federal or state, but organizational structure and procedures may vary from state to state. One must first determine whether the court is federal or state, and then if it is a state court one must understand its position within the state's judicial system. Lack of awareness of the separation between the two court systems [2] and of variations in state judicial systems is at the heart of the misunderstanding about the courts' operation.

Passive Role

The courts have largely a passive role. Unlike legislators and executives, state courts do not take up major policy questions on their own initiative. They do not actively campaign for popular support for their positions. They wait for a litigant to bring a question to them which, under the statutes and the courts' rules, is legitimately presented to them for adjudication. An act of the legislature, for instance, is not considered by a state court unless its legitimacy under the constitution is challenged, or frequently, unless there is a conflict between a state agency and a private citizen or corporation as to its applicability. One who alleges he has been unjustifiably damaged by an official action may challenge that action before the courts. Only then will the court have before it a question that it can pronounce upon. Of the thousands of such questions presented to the court comparatively few involve policy questions. Most simply involve the enforcement of established legal norms—determining the guilt of one alleged to have violated the law, enforcing contractual relationships, determining fault in a damage suit, and the like. In all of these cases, however, the court waits for the private party or public official to bring the question before it; the court does not entertain such questions on its own initiative.

The courts also depend on other agencies to enforce their pro-

---

[2] The state courts are bound by declarations of the federal courts in their interpretation of the laws of the United States or of the Constitution, and in cases of apparent conflict between federal and state laws.

nouncements. Although some courts still exercise the power of contempt and can punish those who do not do as directed, the usual procedure is for courts to rely on the executive for enforcing judicial orders. Likewise, the courts rely on the legislature for determining jurisdiction, authorizing action in certain kinds of proceedings, and determining the structure of the judicial system, including tenure of members, compensation, procedure for selection, and all the details of the system. The state courts are dependent upon the more overtly political policymaking units, the legislature and the executive. To fail to recognize the passive nature of the courts, or to overemphasize their power in making decisions on major questions of public policy is to distort reality, to suggest a far more aggressive role for the courts than they actually exercise and to overestimate their impact on the political life of the society.

Differences in Access

We have emphasized that ease of access to policymakers is an important indicator of their representativeness. This is also true of judicial policymakers. Interest groups often find it desirable, sometimes because they are unable to compete effectively in the other governmental branches, to transfer to the courts their attempts to modify policy. After the legislature has declared broad general policy, and the administrative branch has implemented it, those affected may turn to the courts for a determination of its appropriateness or the correctness of its administrative application. Representatives of political interest groups, like their counterparts in the administration and legislature, attempt to obtain determinations favorable to them. Even though the discussion is not of electoral implications and economic and social repercussions but rather of constitutionalism, justice, common law, reasonableness, and due process, the goal is still the same. The point of contention is whether the policy should be applied to a particular person or group in a particular way to produce a particular result.

Access to the courts, however, differs markedly from access to the other policymaking arenas. It cannot be attained as easily or through the same techniques as to the legislature or the executive. No representative of an interest group can directly approach a state or local judge to try to influence him in his decision; he would probably find himself held in contempt of court, or, if he is a lawyer, disbarred or at least unwelcome before that court in the future. His influence on the court can be made effective only through the prescribed forms and procedures peculiar to the courts. A counsellor may file briefs and engage in oral arguments, but there will be no open debate, no committee hearings, and no invitation for compromise as in a legislative chamber. Introducing evidence in a legal proceeding differs from arguing a point before a legislative committee. Court procedures are couched in the language of the law rather than of politics: judges hear litigants, not interest groups; they consider cases, not programs; they produce decisions (usually only the highest court of the state actually puts its decisions in writing), not statutes.

Although access to the courts is restricted, it is not impossible to obtain. The most effective means for access to the judiciary is the test case, through which those interested in challenging an established policy seek to have a court invalidate or modify it. Litigants are often joined by *amicus curiae*, a "friend of the court," who, though not a party to the case, files a brief in support of one side. Such access is not limited to large organized interest groups. Even an individual can sometimes bring about a change in policy through the courts. However, his access will be through professionals—the lawyers—and his role in influencing the court will be specifically prescribed by its rules.

Such procedures restrict the courts in their policymaking role. The form of consideration—the antagonistic proceeding between interested parties, one of whom claims that the action of the other has adversely affected him—seriously limits those who operate within the judicial arena. Furthermore, the courts' jurisdiction is defined by the state legislature. Consequently, the kinds of cases that can be heard by state courts is controlled by political considerations reflected in the legislature.

Structure and Organization

The fact that different states have widely varying organizational structures for their legal system has already been noted. Two things appear to be uniform throughout the states: first, while we may refer to "state" and "local" courts all states have an hierarchical structure for their courts. All courts are state courts; even the lowest is a part of the state judiciary. Thus there is really no "local" court; it is simply the lowest level of the state judicial system. The structure of the state courts is characterized by a centralized judicial function and an extreme decentralization of the agencies responsible for carrying it out. Second, the variations in structure are determined largely through politics; in other words, variations in court structure reflect the variations in political interest groups and their effectiveness. Courts are added and eliminated not by applying a generally accepted principle of sound organization but as a response to political pressure. The state legislature determines the structure of the judicial system, and it treats the courts essentially as it treats all other matters—decisions relative to them are made by reconciling various interests. Hence it is impossible to speak of either *the* organizational-structural pattern for a state court system or the *best* organizational-structural pattern.

Courts of Limited Jurisdiction

Notwithstanding the wide variety of court systems it is still possible to sketch the typical structural pattern for a state judiciary. Names will vary, as will the complexity of the system. Some states have a simplified three-layered structure, while others have an extremely complicated structure with many layers, each having widely varying jurisdictions. Typically at the lowest level are the local courts, generally trial courts of limited jurisdiction—justices of the peace, local magistrates, police judges, or municipal courts. Often in the past these courts were staffed with officials who were not legally trained, and this is still the practice in the local courts of some states. Where they have been more formalized, they are often called municipal courts, courts of general sessions, or courts of common pleas, and are presided over by legally trained judges. Usually these courts deal with the vast number of traffic cases, small claims, and misdemeanors punishable with small fines or very limited sentences.

Three observations concerning these local courts should be made. First, they handle the majority of most citizens' legal problems, and in most instances the citizens' contact with the court will be through one of them, principally a traffic court. Second, justice in these courts is likely to be quite casual and to vary considerably and noticeably with the predispositions, biases, and experience (or inexperience) of the presiding magistrate. Third, these courts are the ones most closely identified with prevailing political arrangements; they may be staffed with political appointees and may be quite responsive to the interests of dominant politicians.

Courts of General Jurisdiction

At the heart of the judicial system in all states are the courts of "first instance," the trial courts of general jurisdiction. These courts have various names—superior, chancery, circuit, district, or combinations of these—and are the ones that try most of the civil and criminal cases arising out of the ordinances or statutes, common law, or constitutional law of the state. In hearing such cases these courts interpret and apply the state law. Consequently, these courts are tremendously important not only to the individual but also to the development of major policy. Most cases heard by these trial courts are not appealed, and thus for most litigants they are the court of final resort; they make definitive judgments that affect the economic, social, or political future of the persons involved.

High Courts

At the apex of the state court system is the court of last resort. Again, the name varies—supreme court, supreme court of errors, supreme judicial court, supreme court of appeals, court of appeals, and the like—but in every case this is the high court of the state. It sits without a jury, and most of its work is directed to it from the lower courts, although most state supreme courts have some original jurisdiction, and some of them may be appealed to by administrative agencies for advisory opinions on the constitutionality or meaning of a statute. This is the court of last resort except in cases where a federal question is involved; in such instances there may be recourse to the Supreme Court of the United States.

At this level the political impact of decisions have the most apparent and easily recognized importance, for this court makes final determinations of the meaning of state statutes, the constitutionality of state laws and local ordinances, and the meaning of the state constitution. It is not, however, the most important court for the ordinary litigant, who usually does not get beyond the courts of first instance. Also, the overwhelming majority of cases heard by the high court contain no far-reaching policy decisions, being limited to rather esoteric and technical points of law that are of concern essentially only to individual litigants and possibly to those similarly situated as well.

Other Courts

This tripartite hierarchy—local courts of limited jurisdiction, trial courts of general jurisdiction, and the high court—prevails in all states. Some states, however, have auxiliary courts that do not fit neatly into this pattern. The most significant and common of these are of two types: first, special courts at the local level to supplement either local or trial courts. These are set up to deal with specific types of cases such as domestic relations, juveniles, probate, and small claims. They are most common in the larger cities of the more populous states where the amount of business before the courts tends to justify a special court for these matters. Second, in 14 states there are intermediate appellate courts between the trial courts and high court. As their name suggests, they are designated to receive appeals from trial courts and to settle them without the necessity of recourse to the high court. In all cases considered by the appellate courts, however, there is a right of appeal to the high court.

In some of the larger cities trial courts máy be organized into divisions, such as criminal and civil, and sometimes one court will have several divisions of general jurisdiction because the press of business makes it otherwise impossible to handle all the cases brought before it. In almost all states there are also some administrative tribunals that have a quasi-judicial function such as tax or rate adjudications, local zoning, licensing, health and sanitary regulation; although, strictly speaking, they are not courts, nevertheless they are an important adjunct to the judicial system.

For the citizen all of these courts may be important, and for the student of politics each has its own significance both as a part of the judicial system and a part of the state political process. Each of them, even the lowest, makes decisions that potentially affect the life of individuals and the society. We look to the highest appellate courts for decisions on major social, economic, and political problems that have the greatest impact on the greatest number, and which thus most apparently affect the political system; however, lower courts begin the process of decision, and in most cases their ruling is final (is not appealed) and remains as the authoritative judgment or decision.

Selection and Responsibility

There are two general ways to select judges of state courts—by election or appointment. Approximately three of every four choose judges by election. Half of these have a partisan election, and the other half has a nonpartisan election (party affiliations are not on the ballot). In five states judges are elected by the legislature; seven have appointment procedures; and six, some variety of the Missouri Plan in which a special commission recommends candidates to the governor who selects those to be submitted in a referendum to the electorate for their approval.[3] Some states combine methods, electing lower court judges and appointing high court justices.

The question whether judges should be elected or appointed has

[3] In California the system is somewhat different; the governor appoints certain judges without recommendation from a commission, but his appointment must be approved by a special commission, and the judges do not come up for referendum until the expiration of their first term.

been heatedly and widely debated for many years. The usual argument for appointment is that this will insulate the appointees from politics by making it unnecessary for a judge to participate in political affairs to win an election, and that the general public is not able to make a decision as to comparative competence in legal matters.

Regardless of which position one is inclined to support several important points must be taken into account. First, the assumption that appointment removes judges from politics is simply not supported by the evidence. While it may be easily assumed that an appointive system is less "politically" oriented than an electoral system, serious questions may be raised about the validity of this assumption. Although an election normally requires an individual to have political identification, exposure, and fairly extensive experience, it is probably true that a person normally would not be "available" for appointment to the courts without similar experience and exposure. The easy assumption that appointments will be made from the "professionally qualified" and that elections will attract only the "politically oriented" overlooks the probability that the same kinds of experience and qualification will be important to success in either mode of access to a judicial appointment. While elections have the most obvious relationship to politics, appointment, no matter by whom, is not demonstrably less politically involved. Indeed, while it may be easier for a governor to consider nonpolitical characteristics in selecting judiciary appointments, there is nothing in the system requiring him to do so, and in fact, the political system seems to promote political considerations even if he is concerned about professional qualifications of a candidate. Furthermore, we lack evidence of the effect of party affiliation after a justice takes his seat on the bench.

Second, even if one assumes the appointment process can reflect more accurately the qualities of legal competence, this might not be the most important characteristic of appointees to the courts. One whose political positions are clear might be a more reasonable choice than the legally competent specialist because positions of the former are known and his responsiveness to social and political problems is more nearly predictable, whereas the latter's responsiveness relative to such problems might be an indeterminate factor. Serious questions can be raised about which is more important—legal skills and experience or political skills and experience. Both may be desirable, and neither election nor appointment guarantees the correct mix.

Third, only in recent years have we begun to obtain reliable information based on empirical research about the comparative effects of appointment and election. While these data are becoming more plentiful it is too early to assert that they point definitively toward

the superiority of either method. That the methods do make a difference in the kinds of judges who are selected seems to be established,
but those differences are in social and political backgrounds and not
in superior and inferior competence.

Fourth, there is a very strong tradition of judicial objectivity and
nonpolitical involvement. This tradition, perhaps more than selection
methods, helps to insure moderation in the more obvious forms of
political involvement by justices. Some have referred to the "taught
tradition of the law" as a significant influence on the courts, and to
ignore this would be to overlook the expectations of the public that
the courts, both elected and appointed, operate as nonpolitical, nonpartisan arbiters.

Fifth, the limitations on political access to the courts, discussed
above, serve to restrict political involvement in their workings. Thus
judges have a greater degree of immunity to political pressure and
retaliation than the executive and legislator enjoy.

This discussion may be summarized by emphasizing that judges
are major participants in the struggle for political power and the
distribution of rewards from such power. Their decisions affect the
political careers of many people and potentially the economic and
social welfare of most people, and thus they are important repositories
of political power. Any effort to remove them from politics will fail
and, more importantly, may be itself a pathological ingredient in the
democratic policymaking process. Failure to understand the essential
political nature of the judicial process may lead, at best, to frustration
and disappointment as efforts to depoliticize the courts necessarily
fail and, at worst, to the serious mistake of prescribing remedies for
imagined ills.

Some Important Contemporary Problems

The six problem areas discussed below are representative of the
major areas of criticism and concern by observers of the courts. The
reader should consider his particular state and local courts to determine to what extent these kinds of problems exist there.

The most important problem is the general lack of understanding
about the courts and their roles. Professionals—lawyers, judges, and
students of the courts—are by no means ignorant of the judicial
process, but they have less empirical research about the courts than
is available about the other governmental units discussed in this
volume. Absence of empirical data is of concern to students of the
courts. In addition, the general lack of understanding and knowledge

about the courts by the citizen not only reflects this dearth of data and research but also is partially responsible for it. There is an aura of mystery surrounding the courts, suggesting they should be beyond the normal reach of the researcher, unapproachable, unlike a legislative committee or an executive agency. Adding to this is the unintelligible (to all but specialists) language and procedures of the courts. The operation of the courts is meaningful to the citizen only after interpretation by a professional. Not only does this insulate the courts from the citizen and promote the indispensability of the lawyer as an agent for even the simplest legal problems of the citizen, but also, more importantly, it reinforces his ignorance about one of the most important policymaking and conflict-resolving agencies of the state.

Another really difficult problem is delay. As our population increases and concentrates in the urban areas the problem of crowded court dockets—too many cases with too few courts to hear them—continues to become more critical. It is not unusual at all for a case, such as a personal injury suit, to take one to four years to make its way through the court of original jurisdiction. Frequently criminal cases are not heard until months after the charge is initially brought against the accused. Some efforts to recover damages are virtually meaningless by the time the cases are settled. Solutions have been suggested, and many have been tried, but as the society becomes more heavily populated and more technologically and scientifically oriented, the legal questions tend to increase, and the problems for the courts become greater. Justice delayed may be justice denied.

The availability and cost of legal assistance are also of concern. Legal processes are expensive. While in theory and law the courts are available to all who need them and have a legitimate claim under the statutes, many citizens cannot avail themselves of the judicial process because of the high costs involved. Even though many states and local communities have begun programs for legal assistance to the indigent, there is a large percentage of Americans who, though not indigent, are unable to afford the best legal advice and counsel. Since success in the courts is affected by the attorneys' skill, an inability to hire the most competent attorney may seriously restrict one's chances of success.

The lack of expertise of those who sit on our state and local benches is of major concern. If the courts exercise a significant role in both conflict adjudication and policymaking their competence to do so is obviously of major concern. Yet there is little or no evidence that they have any particular claim to competence in making policy. There is little comfort in supposing jurists are no less competent than their counterparts in the legislature and executive branch, for the definitive-ness of their decisions suggests that a lack of special expertness in the courts is more difficult to compensate for. Furthermore, often a court is asked to make a decision on a technical matter of policy about which it can make no claim to expertise, yet court procedures often preclude having the kind of expert assistance commonly available to the legislator through interest groups that testify before the committees. Counsel briefs and *amicus curiae* may partially compensate for this lack, but the insulation of the courts from direct access handicaps them in obtaining competent advice on technical matters of policy.

Trial by jury is guaranteed by the Constitution of the United States and reinforced by state constitutions. Juries date back to the medieval origins of our legal system and were brought to this country from England. Trial by jury today is largely a thing of the past, more and more cases being heard by a judge alone. But the affection for it has not diminished. The suggestion that trial by jury is not indispensable to justice in our courts is received with considerable alarm by most audiences. However, the evidence has begun to accumulate; juries are not representative of the peers of the accused or of the community. Most lawyers, ministers, teachers, professionals of all kinds, and housewives are usually excused from jury service. Indeed, often it seems as though all those who know anything about the case or who have qualities fitting them to understand the complexity of the law and the legal process are excused from sitting on the jury. What is left is hardly a cross section of the population. And one can hardly assume that the average jury is competent to understand the complex problems of the law and the technicalities that are a part of the trial.

Similar difficulties reside in the grand jury. It precedes the trial jury and has two primary duties. The first is to indict, that is, bring to trial, those accused of violating the law when there is probable cause to justify such a trial. In many states this function has been replaced by indictment through the "information," a document submitted to the court by the prosecuting attorney demonstrating why the individual should be called to trial. The second function of the grand jury is largely investigatory; it serves as a kind of public conscience, making broad investigations into alleged or real malfeasance in office, immorality, crime, and legal problems requiring the attention of either the courts or the local legislature. In most cases it is composed of a rather large number of members, sometimes as many as 23, who are normally laymen qualified for the post by a combination of political connections, a name of prestige, and ample time to sit on the grand jury. This may be the least understood of the governmental institutions at the local level, but it is undoubtedly one of those with the greatest support. Many scholars have said that its day is past; however in most local communities it is highly unlikely that it could be easily eliminated. If there is a need for an agency to oversee local government, to check on the responsibility and legality of officials' actions, or to ferret out real or imagined areas needing remedial attention, better means can be devised than to rely on this ancient institution.

In Conclusion

In the last three chapters we have examined the three major governmental arenas and their roles in the policymaking process. The legislature, the executives and administrators, and the judiciary have been discussed individually and independently for convenience and clarity. Now it remains for the reader to consider these three areas together, to develop his understanding of the relationships among them, and to apply the general analysis of democratic theory and the political system developed in Chapters 3 and 4. If he studies the institutions separately and fails to apply the general theory of the nature of democracy and the specifics of political involvement, his understanding of our state and local units as part of the political system will be deficient and misleading. That task remains for him both in the study of state and local government and in his role as a citizen.

Guide to Further Reading*

General. There is no lack of textbooks on state and local government. Few, however, are of more than minimal interest. Among the more useful are Daniel R. Grant and H. C. Nixon, *State and Local Government in America* (Boston: Allyn and Bacon, Inc., 2nd ed., 1968), probably the best general text; James W. Fesler, ed., *The 50 States and Their Local Communities* (New York: Alfred A. Knopf, Inc., 1967), a collection of excellent contributions by eight of the best state and local scholars; Duane Lockard, *The Politics of State and Local Government* (New York: The Macmillan Company, 1963), now somewhat dated but notable for its emphasis on politics; Russell W. Maddox and Robert F. Fuquay, *State and Local Government* (Princeton: D. Van Nostrand Company, Inc., 2nd ed., 1966), a useful encyclopedic volume; and Russell M. Ross and Kenneth F. Millsap, *State and Local Government and Administration* (New York: The Ronald Press Company, 1966), with a heavy emphasis on administrative aspects.

General texts limited to state government are best represented by John C. Buechner, *State Government in the Twentieth Century* (Boston: Houghton Mifflin Company, 1967). City government has come in for much attention, and the best general treatments are Charles R. Adrian, *Governing Urban America* (New York: McGraw-Hill, Inc., 2d ed., 1961), now dated but extremely useful; and Edward C. Banfield and James Q. Wilson, *City Politics* (Cambridge: Harvard University Press, 1963), a deliberately political approach to urban government.

Still the most useful collection of readings are two volumes by Charles Press and Oliver P. Williams, *Democracy in the Fifty States* (Chicago: Rand McNally & Company, 1966) and *Democracy in Urban America* (Chicago: Rand McNally & Company, 1961).

An indispensable general reference is *The Book of the States* (Chicago: Council of State Governments), an annual compilation of enormous amounts of data about all aspects of state government.

Systems Analysis. Easton's volume, footnoted in Chapter 1, is by far the most useful, but H. V. Wiseman, *Political Systems: Some Socio-*

---

* Also see the publications mentioned in footnotes in the chapters, which are not generally repeated here.

logical Approaches (New York: Frederick A. Praeger, Publishers, 1966) is an excellent and thorough consideration of the systems approach. More abbreviated explanations of the systems approach are David Easton, "An Approach to the Analysis of Political Systems," *World Politics*, 9 (1956–57), 383–400; and Herbert Jacob, "State Political Systems," in Herbert Jacob and Kenneth N. Vines, eds., *Politics in the American States* (Boston: Little, Brown and Company, 1965), pp. 3–21.

Constitution. References on constitutions and constitutionalism are legion. Perhaps most useful here would be Arthur N. Holcombe, *The Constitutional System* (Chicago: Scott, Foresman and Company, 1964); Charles Black Jr., *Perspectives on Constitutional Law* (Englewood Cliffs, N.J.: Prentice-Hall, Inc., 1963; and D. W. Brogan, *Politics in America* (New York: Harper and Brothers, 1954), Chap. 1, "The Character of the American Polity," an incisive discussion of the central role constitutions play in American experience.

Intergovernmental Relations. Federalism is considered from many viewpoints in Robert A. Goldman, ed., *A Nation of States: Essays on the American Federal System* (Chicago: Rand McNally & Company, 1963), including seven essays by leading students of our federal system. Other useful books include William H. Riker, *Federalism: Origin, Operation, Significance* (Boston: Little, Brown and Company, 1964); and Valerie Earle, *Federalism: Infinite Variety in Theory and Practice* (Itasca, Ill.: F. E. Peacock Publishers, Inc., 1968); and Daniel J. Elazar, *American Federalism: A View from the States* (New York: Thomas Y. Crowell Company, 1966).

Metropolitan government and politics has preoccupied many scholars in recent years, with a consequent deluge of references, many repetitive and of little real value. Among the better are the following: John C. Bollens and Henry J. Schmandt, *The Metropolis: Its People, Politics, and Economic Life* (New York: Harper & Row, 1965), a near-encyclopedic volume; Scott Greer, *Governing the Metropolis* (New York: John Wiley & Sons, Inc., 1962); and Jeffrey K. Hadden, et al., *Political Perspectives* (Itasca, Ill.: F. E. Peacock Publishers, Inc., 1967), an excellent compilation of major readings bearing on the metropolis. One of the most incisive studies is Scott Greer, *Metropolitics: A Study of Political Culture* (New York: John Wiley & Sons, Inc., 1963).

Theoretical Framework of Politics. Robert A. Dahl has contributed several important works to the development of a realistic theory of democracy upon which this volume rests. Particularly helpful are his

A Preface to Democratic Theory (Chicago: University of Chicago Press, 1956) and *Modern Political Analysis* (Englewood Cliffs, N.J.: Prentice-Hall, Inc., 1963). A provocative challenge to the restatement of democratic theory is found in Lane Davis, "The Cost of Realism: Contemporary Restatements of Democracy," *The Western Political Quarterly*, XVII, 1 (March, 1964), 37–46. A most useful compilation of sources is M. Rejai, *Democracy: The Contemporary Theories* (New York: Atherton Press, 1967). Almost alone in the field is Anwar Syed, *The Political Theory of American Local Governments* (New York: Random House, Inc., 1966). A convenient source for reference to many of the scholars contributing to contemporary theory of democracy is Leonard J. Fein, *American Democracy: Essays on Image and Realities* (New York: Holt, Rinehart & Winston, Inc., 1964).

The classic reference on political parties and interest groups is V. O. Key, *Politics, Parties and Pressure Groups* (New York: Thomas Y. Crowell Company, 5th ed., 1964). A most useful series of essays is included in Robert A. Goldwin, ed., *Political Parties, U.S.A.* (Chicago: Rand McNally & Company, 1964).

State and Local Politics. By far the best analysis of state politics is found in Herbert Jacob and Kenneth N. Vines, eds., *Politics in the American States* (Boston: Little, Brown and Company, 1965), especially Part II, "Participation in State Politics," including considerations of voter participation, parties, and interest groups. An interesting comparative approach is represented in the readings in Frank Munger, ed., *American State Politics: Readings for Comparative Analysis* (New York: Thomas Y. Crowell Company, 1966). Another excellent collection of readings is Robert E. Crew, Jr., *State Politics: Readings on Political Behavior* (Belmont, Calif.: Wadsworth Publishing Company, Inc., 1968.

Excellent examples of the many fine casebooks on urban politics are Gladys M. Kammerer, et al., *The Urban Political Community: Profiles in Town Politics* (Boston: Houghton Mifflin Company, 1963), and Edward C. Banfield, *Political Influence* (New York: The Free Press, 1961), a study of the way influence works in a large American city. Another essential reference is M. Kent Jennings, *Community Influentials: The Elites of Atlanta* (New York: The Free Press, 1964). A superb collection of the sources on community power is Willis D. Hawley and Frederick M. Wirt, eds., *The Search for Community Power* (Englewood Cliffs, N.J.: Prentice-Hall, Inc., 1968), including those of the Lynds, Hunter, Dahl, Wildavsky, Sayre, and many others. Edward C. Banfield, *Big City Politics* (New York: Random House, Inc., 1965), provides the only available comparative study of the politics of Atlanta, Boston, Detroit, El Paso, Los Angeles, Miami, Philadelphia, St. Louis, and Seattle. Big-city machine politics is discussed by Edward J. Flynn, twenty-five-year "boss of the Bronx," in *You're the Boss: The Practice of American Politics* (New York: The Crowell-Collier Publishing Company, 1962).

Legislatures and Policymaking. A useful short consideration of the policymaking process may be found in Charles E. Lindblom, *The Policy-Making Process* (Englewood Cliffs, N.J.: Prentice-Hall, Inc., 1968). Part 3, "The Policy-Making Arenas," of Jacob & Vines, *op. cit.*, presents outstanding analyses of legislative, executive, and judicial politics and policymaking. Specific considerations of state and local legislatures can usually be obtained easily only from general textbooks; no definitive study of these legislatures is available. The most convenient source for materials on legislative reapportionment is Glendon Schubert, *Reapportionment* (New York: Charles Scribner's Sons, 1965), an anthology including articles and materials on all aspects of the problem.

Executives and Administrators. Essential background reading includes Chester I. Barnard, *The Functions of the Executive* (Cambridge: Harvard University Press, 1954). An excellent theoretical consideration of the problem of representation is found in Heinz Eulau, et al., "The Role of the Representative: Some Empirical Observations on the Theory of Edmund Burke," *American Political Science Review*, LIII, 3 (September, 1959), 742–56. A near-classic is Herman Finer, "Administrative Responsibility in Democratic Government," *Public Administration Review*, 1 (Summer, 1941), 335–50. There are no studies of state and local executives meriting attention except those found in the general textbooks previously noted. Perhaps the best will be found in Jacob and Vines, *op. cit.*

The Judiciary. General textbooks and the Jacob and Vines volume supply our best discussions of state and local courts. Henry J. Abraham, *The Judicial Process* (New York: Oxford University Press, 1962) is an excellent reference on the judicial system in general and supplies a wealth of information of use to the student of state and local courts. Several chapters in Herbert Jacob, *Justice in America: Courts, Lawyers, and the Judicial Process* (Boston: Little, Brown and Company, 1965) are informative, particularly Chap. 1, "Courts in the Political Arena," and Chap. 3, "Policy-Making by the Courts." Kenneth Vines has done extensive research on the state courts; his articles in various journals are among the best sources available.

Index